"Understanding spiritual discernment was never so much fun!"

In my Christian life I have tried to help everyone who needs help and to be kind to everyone I come in contact with. I have found, though, that not everyone who comes to me comes for help. Some come to destroy and spread dissension. It is in these cases we must ask for God's direction and discernment. Little is said in the Christian community about how to identify or what to do with those whose direction is destruction. Prior to *Kingdom Zoology*, we were guided only by a feeling in our stomach. With his usual quick wit, Joel Freeman presents an entertaining case for spiritual discernment.

Florence Littauer
Author and Speaker

In his usual entertaining but provocative style, Joel Freeman introduces us to the "animals" that make kingdom living so difficult and dangerous for all of us. The new believer as well as the seasoned saint will both find a great deal of practical biblical counsel in these fascinating chapters.

Warren W. Wiersbe
Author and Bible Teacher

Joel Freeman is unique in his ability to communicate biblical truth in creative ways. In this challenging book, Joel provides every Christian with the vital information needed to develop their own spiritual discernment as they seek to evaluate and maintain quality in Christian relationships. Understanding spiritual discernment was never so much fun!

Dr. Anthony T. Evans
Senior Pastor
Oak Cliff Bible Fellowship

"All the world's a zoo," says Joel Freeman, slightly revising Shakespeare. For Christians, it seems, "All the church is a zoo," if I might revise Freeman. God, of course, is the zoo's Grand Curator who will, in time, revise us all. This is Freeman's promise and he keeps that promise in *Kingdom Zoology*. So find your own cage, let God in, read and be revised; it's for your own good.

Calvin Miller
Author, *The Singer Trilogy*
Pastor, Westside Church

Peter says that some people behave like animals. They "act by instinct, like wild animals." All of us are capable of acting like animals, not as men and women made in the image of God. In *Kingdom Zoology*, Joel Freeman has a sharp eye for brutish behavior, and in this colorful book he warns us to watch out for it.

Donald Cole
Radio Pastor
Moody Broadcasting Network

Kingdom Zoology

JOEL A. FREEMAN

Here's Life Publishers

First Printing, August 1991

Published by
HERE'S LIFE PUBLISHERS, INC.
P. O. Box 1576
San Bernardino, CA 92402

Cover design by David Marty Design
Cover illustrations by Bruce Day

Library of Congress Cataloging-in-Publication Data
Freeman, Joel A., 1954-
    Kingdom zoology : dealing with the wolves, serpents and
swine in your life / Joel A. Freeman.
        p.   cm.
    ISBN 0-89840-327-8
    1. Christian life—1960- . 2. Interpersonal relations—
Religious aspects—Christianity. I. Title.
BV4501.2.F758   1991
248.4—dc20   91-631
                          CIP

Unless indicated otherwise, Scripture quotations are from the *King James Version*.

Scripture quotations designated NIV are from *The Holy Bible: New International Version*, © 1973, 1978, 1984 by the International Bible Society. Published by Zondervan Bible Publishers, Grand Rapids, Michigan.

Scripture quotations designated TEV are from *The Good News Bible: Today's English Version*, © 1966, 1971, 1976 by the American Bible Society. Published by Thomas Nelson Publishers, Nashville, Tennessee.

The concept of five fools was borrowed from *The Doctrine of Fools*, © 1984 by Joel A. Freeman.

Unless specifically identified as factual, all names have been fictionalized for protection and privacy.

For More Information, Write:

L.I.F.E.—P.O. Box A399, Sydney South 2000, Australia
Campus Crusade for Christ of Canada—Box 300, Vancouver, B.C., V6C 2X3, Canada
Campus Crusade for Christ—Pearl Assurance House, 4 Temple Row, Birmingham, B2 5HG, England
Lay Institute for Evangelism—P.O. Box 8786, Auckland 3, New Zealand
Campus Crusade for Christ—P.O. Box 240, Raffles City Post Office, Singapore 9117
Great Commission Movement of Nigeria—P.O. Box 500, Jos, Plateau State Nigeria, West Africa
Campus Crusade for Christ International—Arrowhead Springs, San Bernardino, CA 92414, U.S.A.

Dedicated to my brother and friend
Stephen T. Freeman

Okay, okay, I admit it.
While you were gone, I did sneak into your room
and touch your stuff on March 3, 1961.

Acknowledgments

To God. Your mercies are new every morning. Thank You . . .

Special thanks to my wonderful wife, Laurie, and my sons, David and Jesse, for your support and understanding. You are a part of everything I am and do. I have been blessed with a great family!

Thanks to each and every member of Stillmeadow Christian Fellowship for allowing me to take time away from you to write and travel. You have captured a vision of the power of the printed page. You are a wild and crazy bunch!

Thanks to Madeline Harrington. You were able to translate my "chicken scratchings" into legible copy. I still don't know how you did it.

Thanks to Dan Benson, my editorial director, and Barbara Sherrill, the project editor. You both have been blessed with the ability to take an imperfect manuscript and increase its life-changing quality. You are the best!

Thanks to Dawn Dicker for proofreading this book and for making valuable corrections and suggestions.

Contents

Foreword

by Chuck Smith

Kingdom Zoology is well written, easy to understand and well supported by Scripture. Joel Freeman's unique style of humor along with numerous practical illustrations certainly capture the reader's attention.

The book delivers a balanced presentation on how to understand and deal with the many problem individuals one confronts along the Christian road of life that the Bible labels as wolves, swine, serpents and dogs, etc. *Kingdom Zoology* challenges the reader to examine his or her own wolf-like characteristics.

Scratching Where You Itch

If you're itching, the book you now hold in your hands is scratching. In this volume, I am addressing two needs that confront every one of us. Put yourself in these scenarios and see if you feel a wee bit itchy:

ITCH #1: "I have been scammed, ripped-off and used by some of the seemingly nicest people. In fact, I'm not sure I want to deal with so-called Christians anymore. It seems like they're always looking for a good-brother discount, or they borrow something and don't return it, or they smile, expecting me to forgive them for repeated failures. I have had enough.

"I need to develop a better sense of spiritual discernment in terms of who I choose to spend my time with. I want to be able to spot people who are wolf-like, swine-like or serpent-like in their behavior. At the same time I want to be able to spot those who are committed to sheep-like behavior. The bottom line is that I want to be wise in the ways of the Lord. And I'd like to apply that wisdom to my relationships with people: Who I do business with. Who I marry. Who I help. Who I choose to groom for leadership responsibilities. Get the picture?"

ITCH #2: "In the same breath, I don't want to be a wolf or a swine to someone else. I am painfully aware of my own tendency to behave wrongly toward others, especially when a so-called friend has caused me emotional pain. At times, I have been frightened by the depths of rage and my almost uncontrollable desire to lash out at those who hurt me. I want to be pure in heart. I don't want to impede the progress of others by being a stumbling block. I'm not perfect, but one thing I'm certain about: I want to avoid wolf-like attitudes or behavior, whatever they may be."

Are you starting to itch? Turn the page and continue reading. Learn how to deal with wolves without becoming one yourself. The words just might start scratching where you itch.

Joel A. Freeman, Ph.D.
5110 Frederick Avenue
Baltimore, Maryland 21229

Animated Animalism

The church is something like Noah's ark.
If it weren't for the storm outside, you couldn't
stand the smell inside.
—Anonymous

I like cartoons. Mickey Mouse. Donald Duck. Woody Woodpecker. Road Runner. The Coyote. Porky Pig. Bugs Bunny.

"Hey, what's up, Doc?"

"W-Well, I guess w-what attracts me to cartoons is th-that so many of th-them are about animals th-that behave l-like human beings."

Well said. Thanks for your perspective, Porky. It's so true. I laugh when Donald Duck gets flustered about something. His reactions are so human-like. It's funny to watch the Road Runner bait the trap for the Coyote. I get a vicarious thrill every time he falls off a cliff. His fixation with the Road Runner causes him to lose touch with reality. The Coyote is so stupid sometimes—just like us humans.

On the flipside, however, there is a grim reality—humans that behave like animals. Sly, like a fox. Proud, like a peacock. Stubborn, like a mule. Waiting to strike, like a snake in the grass.

One begins to wonder if there is anybody out there who truly has the best interests of others at heart. Are there any candidates? How about someone who behaves like a sheep?

Recently, I performed a wedding ceremony on a large party boat. It was a fancy schmancy, black-tie event that cruised out of Baltimore's Inner Harbor. During the course of the afternoon, I met a fascinating man. He was in his late fifties. He had sparkling eyes that communicated a mixture of hard living and boyish mischief. I primed the pump and sat back to listen to this self-made man I'll call Taylor.

He had a no-nonsense, rough edge to him. With spicy language he told stories about gun deals he had made with anti-government, terrorist-type men in Central and South America through the years. As a pilot with a private plane, Taylor had carved out quite a niche for himself in the seedy underworld of on-the-edge-of-your-seat danger and millions of dollars. It didn't take long for me to realize that his life experience was excellent grist for the movie mill. It was almost unbelievable.

"I was in El Salvador doing a deal," he said. "We all had pistols stuffed in our belts. I knew that any one of those men could blow me away in an instant. Yet I felt safer there than if I was on the main street of my hometown. I turned to those guys and pointed to each one saying, 'Listen, I'm an s.o.b., you're an s.o.b., you're an s.o.b., you're an s.o.b. and you're an s.o.b. Now that we all know what we are, let's do business.' "

Taylor laughed enthusiastically and then paused. He looked intently into my eyes.

"Joel, it's not the s.o.b.'s. of the world you have to watch out for," he said. "You always know where you stand with them. It's the do-gooders you have to be careful about. They'll smile to your face and then stab you when you turn your back."

What Taylor said that day has made me think. When viewed from an earth-bound perspective, his philosophy holds up to the test of reality in many ways. I don't know about your experience, but most of the raw deals I have encountered in life have been per- petrated by the type of people who are prone to slap "I'm Not Perfect, Just Forgiven" bumper stickers on their cars. It could almost make me a semi-paranoid, constantly-looking-over-my-shoulder type of guy. Cynical. Always searching for the dark, shadowy side of people.

I have looked into the tearful eyes of pastors whose reputations have been smeared by other pastors. I've talked with business people who have been stiffed by Christians promising to pay their bills. People in- volved in street ministry have been burned time and time again by ex-cons who got jailhouse religion.

And something saddens me even more when I consider all this. *I* have hurt people in the name of Christianity. *I* have been a perpetrator of heartache. It is almost frightening to realize my own capacity when it comes to evil. Like Taylor said, "It's the do-gooders you have to be careful about."

What's Lurking Under the Sheepskins . . .

Human beings are a puzzle. Just when you think you've got them figured out, one of them does something completely out of character and you're left scratching your head.

Since most of our emotional pain involves people, it is vital for us to understand what's behind their actions and words. That's why I wrote this book. *Kingdom Zoology* is about discernment. It's about you and me. It's the product of much study and heartache in my interactions with various types of people. My prayer is that this book will provide the tools for you to deepen your understanding about dealing with those who have a destructive, evil proclivity.

To a certain extent, this book evolved from the harsh experiences with really only a handful of people. People who, on the surface, had all the appearances of Christian love and character, but later on caused profound damage within the church. With the advantage of hindsight, I can see clearly now that underneath those sheepskins lurked ravenous wolves. Much of what I write has been filtered through tears.

I hope, though, that I never become jaded. The vast majority of church people I have worked with have been wonderful. They love the Word, work hard and patiently put up with my many flagrant displays of immaturity and zeal. Most Christians are terrific people!

My prayer to God through the years has been something like this: "Lord, please protect our church from wolves, pigs, serpents or goats. Just send sheep. I'll take all types. Sick sheep. Grumpy sheep. Neurotic sheep. Sleepy sheep. Happy sheep. Weird sheep. Wounded sheep. Noisy sheep. Boring sheep. Backslidden sheep. White sheep. Black sheep. Well, You get the picture. Thanks for listening."

This book is not written from an ivory tower of perfection. I am hopeful about God's gracious work in *all* our lives. We should not fear taking risks with people who seem to be wolf-like. Nor should we be self-conscious in our relationships with others. It is important, however, for us to be aware of the fact that there are distinctive differences between people when it comes to the motivations of the heart.

If at times my words seem to take on a judgmental tone, remember that behind these sentences beats a merciful heart. It has been said that the most ardent evangelists of the good may be those who have had close encounters with evil.

I love sheep, but sometimes even sheep have sharp teeth.

Points to Ponder

1. Do you, like Taylor, feel that "nice guys" can be the most dangerous? If so, how has that affected your opinion of people in general?

2. Have you noticed "wolf-like" tendencies in yourself? Are you tempted to justify any shortcomings with excuses borrowed from a "dog-eat-dog" philosophy (e.g., "You've gotta look out for #1" or "Nice guys finish last")?

The Swine Test

*Be kind. Remember everyone you meet
is fighting a hard battle.*
—John Watson

It was like a snapshot from hell. One sweltering dog-day in August, three preachers were playing golf as economically as possible by splitting the cost of one golf cart. Smith, Jones and Snickerbum were their names. Taking turns from hole to hole, one would huff and puff his way down the fairway while the other two would tool their way toward the green, allowing the humid air to waft gleefully about their ever-so-few locks of hair.

You've heard of 666, haven't you? Well, how about 6 runs for Smith, 6 runs for Jones and 6 for Snickerbum? They affectionately dubbed the course, The Beast.

After the eighteenth hole, the ecclesiastical trio decided to grab a bite to eat in the air-conditioned comfort of the clubhouse. A fun time was had by all as they reminisced about their separate seminary experiences.

Practical jokes. Snooping dormitory supervisors. Skip-ping classes.

In fact, the somewhat reverent frivolity reached such a crescendo that they started feeling a special closeness with each other. There is, I am told, a rather thin line between laughter and tears. Sometimes people won't let you weep with them until you've laughed with them first.

There was a brief pause in their trip down memory lane. Jones broke the silence. "Gentlemen," he began, while gulping down the last French fry, "I have some-thing to tell you that I have never told another soul." He finished chewing and then cleared his throat.

Smith and Snickerbum leaned forward. Jones hesitated while searching their faces intently. "I have a secret drinking problem," he confided. "I am finally realizing that I am an alcoholic."

You could have heard a pin drop in their remote corner. Jones lowered his eyes, anxiously tracing the checkerboard pattern on the tablecloth with his finger.

Smith felt compelled to speak. "You know," he said, "I also have been struggling with something in my own life that I have never mentioned to another per-son." He felt comfortable now since Jones had already cracked the ice.

"I have a terrible problem with women," Smith went on. "Everywhere I turn, I go crazy with passionate desires. I've tried everything, but nothing seems to help."

Smith and Jones looked up at each other. They had connected. It was like the deep calling to the deep. As if on cue, they turned and looked expectantly to Snicker-bum.

Snickerbum chuckled nervously, averting their

eyes. "Hey, fellows, I have my own problem," he responded. "I am a compulsive gossiper and I can't wait to get out of here!"

I am reminded of an insightful remark from Dr. Donald Joy, author of *Bonding*:

> In your own experience you have probably some-times wondered where you could "bare your soul" when you were experiencing a private kind of grief or hurt. I am amazed that some people can blurt out very personal hurts in a larger group, but most of us need to look around the circle huddled in the narthex or in the parking lot to check the eyes of our listeners. We are checking to see whether we can trust our private grief or pain with these people. I call that caution "the swine test." Jesus, knowing that pearls are formed by painful and uninvited intrusions, warned us not "to cast our pearls before swine." If we open our hearts, we should know that the risk is that the pigs may charge into us viciously, wounding us further and trampling our pearls. I caution my "spiritual formation groups" not to make personal disclosures to the group until they experience a sense of absolute trust and discretion in the room. Don't risk the swine test with your valuable pearls.[1]

As Dr. Joy states, there are those who take the private heartache and pain of others and, for whatever reason, expose it for all to hear and see. Their behavior is almost beastly. Vicious. Heartless. Arrogant.

At the same time, I take a deep breath, realizing that the "Snickerbum," trample-the-pearls tendency lies within me. Immaturity and misguided zeal have motivated me, at times, to put my mouth in gear while my brain was still in neutral.

People-Sheep and People-Pigs

This reflection leads me to make a semi-profound

statement that hitchhikes on a famous quotation: All the world's a zoo. (Eat your heart out, William Shakespeare.) And what a zoo it is! Wolves. Sheep. Foxes. Dogs. Goats. Snakes. Pigs. And more. But how can you tell who's who?

Jesus made that rather shocking statement: "Don't throw your pearls in front of pigs." Just think about it. Jesus is not talking about pig-pigs. He's speaking to people-sheep about two-legged people-pigs. If you were on the scene when He made that statement, wouldn't you want to ask some questions to get more clarity on the subject?

"Jesus," you might ask, "how do I determine whether a person is a pig? And what do I do with that information once I figure it out? How do I guard myself from becoming judgmental in the process? Is there a difference between suspicion and discernment? How do I deal with the animal qualities in me?"

I've done a lot of contemplation on those questions, the result of which you now hold in your hands. But before addressing those issues and more, we need to go back about 2000 years. There we'll find a scene that bears profound implications for your life and mine.

Points to Ponder

1. Who was the person to fail your most recent "swine test"? How did you feel about him or her? Have you ever failed a similar test—unintentionally divulging a confidence, for example?

2. What kind of qualities does a person need in order to pass the swine test? How many of these qualities are evident in your life?

Relative Beings

*What we believe about God
is the most important thing about us.*
—*A. W. Tozer*

Picture the scene: The sun was smoldering as they stood on the rocky shore of the Jordan River at Caesarea Philippi, a tiny village situated at the southwestern lower slope of towering Mount Hermon.

From this vantage point, a person could overlook the fertile north end of the Jordan Valley below. The terrace was well watered by one of the main sources of the river which sprang from a nearby cave.

It was a strategic place, rich in history. This natural site for worship had long ago been dedicated to various Semite deities. In Old Testament times it was probably the hot spot for those who had revered the storm-god, Baal.

The importance of the location was visually enhanced by a shrine that was already ancient when the Greeks had dedicated it to "Pan and the Nymphs," as an inscription testified. Idols were nestled in the niches of a high rock wall.

Jesus squinted as He gazed intently into the eyes of each of His disciples. Amid the setting of rampant paganism, He asked the question, "But who do you say that I am?"

Dramatic silence. Matthew stared off to the distance in deep thought. Looking down, Thomas scuffed the edge of his sandal against a large stone. Bartholomew plucked gently at his beard.

Peter punctuated the stillness with a nervous cough followed by a rather bold statement. "You are the Christ, the Son of the living God," he answered with emotion.

Excitement danced in the Master's voice: "You are blessed, Peter, because flesh and blood did not reveal it to you, but my Father which is in heaven."

Jesus had already taught the disciples about the distinction between darkness and light, life and death, foolishness and wisdom. He had told them that people either gather with Him or join the system which scatters. They knew much about discerning between good and evil.

From Jesus' perspective, there were no gray areas. Humans related either to Satan's kingdom or to God's kingdom. This is the fundamental difference between wolf-like and sheep-like behavior.

When Peter confessed Jesus as the Christ, he was relating to the kingdom of God. Peter didn't conceive of Jesus' identity on his own. After Jesus blessed him, Peter was commended on the basis of the source of his revelation—the Father. Jesus was thrilled because Peter had responded to the right kingdom.

With this scene in mind, let's pause and take a studied look at what happens next.

Jesus graphically describes His approaching suffering, death and resurrection. Peter can't resist. He takes Jesus to the side and says rebukingly, "Oh no, You're not going to die. All these things You've been talking about will not happen to You."

Jesus turns to him with the withering words, "Get thee behind me, Satan." Ouch!

The Essence of True Discernment

Hey, wait a minute! Wasn't Peter motivated by a sincere affection for his Master when he spoke? Wasn't this just another symptom of Foot-in-Mouth disease?

Here's where genuine discernment is needed. True discernment gazes beneath the surface of seemingly harmless words or actions and understands the invisible kingdom issues that have sponsored what is both seen and heard.

Unwittingly, Peter had become a spokesman for a philosophy incubated in hell. Jesus' death ensured Satan's defeat. The shedding of His blood would pay the penalty for every sin—past, present and future. Do you think Lucifer would like that to happen? Absolutely not!

Initially, Peter was a wise man because of his heart's response to God. Jesus commended him for receiving that revelation. Just a short time later, however, he was a fool because he had responded to the wrong kingdom. Jesus wasted no time in exposing the source of Peter's verbalized thoughts—Satan himself.

Wisdom and foolishness have nothing to do with intelligence, social status, financial well-being, education or talent. Our wisdom, or the lack thereof, is determined by which kingdom we relate to. That choice is ours.

I fully realize that there are natural causes involved in the intricacies of human behavior. It is still a riddle how inherited traits, trauma experienced during childhood and personality temperaments can impact a person's behavior. Yet, in the midst of all this, we cannot disregard the fact that spiritual warfare plays an important part in the whole scheme of things.

Spiritual warfare is not a battle over inanimate objects, pieces of real estate or planets in outer space. The focus is on *people*. People like you and me. People who laugh and cry. People of all shapes and sizes. People made of dust, yet with an eternal destiny. People with more questions than answers.

Life in the Battle Zone

Because we're the focus of spiritual warfare, it's going to affect who we are and how we live. We're constantly fighting the battle of which kingdom we relate to.

Have you ever been the object of someone's extreme hatred or vindictiveness? Maybe a neighbor from across the street, a member of the church you attend, a co-worker who harbors secret envy toward you, a relative who has sought to ruin your reputation for no apparent reason.

Slowly but surely, vicious gossip, innuendos and utterly spiteful rumors about your personal life or work habits begin to filter back to you. You discover that they have been circulating around the community for months.

You are perplexed. Who or what is the origin of these fabrications? After careful investigation, you trace it back to one person. Righteous, or should we say, semi-righteous indignation wells up from within. Bitterness tries to plant its ugly seeds in your heart. Revenge attempts to lay claim to a piece of your soul.

After calming down with God's help, you muster up the courage to approach the author of the Peyton Place fiction in a gentle, unassuming manner. You want to discern the motivation behind each uncalled-for assault on your character. But to no avail.

Immediate defensiveness on your attacker's part. You can see it in his eyes and in his body language. The inflection in his voice exhibits profound insecurity. You soon ascertain that he cannot be dealt with on a rational level. He seems to be driven by a bizarre way of thinking that defies common logic. His mind is made up. Don't confuse him with facts.

You feel violated. You approached him in good faith, expecting to be met at least halfway. Instead, he has smugly sabotaged your goodwill gesture. What's your next move? Where do you go from here?

Time passes. The slanderous remarks continue. It becomes abundantly clear that you are dealing with someone who is relating to the system that scatters. He is more comfortable with darkness than he is with the light of truth. His behavior is wolf-like, swine-like. He seems to be controlled by the need to destroy. He will expose the slightest flaw at any cost. And if he can't find a flaw, he will design one.

There is no question now which kingdom he is relating to. But what about you? In your response to this situation, which kingdom has you in their control?

We Are What We Relate To

Like this man, we are relative beings. Our inclinations in behind-the-scenes matters ultimately make up the sum total of our character-who we are and how we function in all our pursuits. We are what we relate to.

When we relate to Satan's earth-bound kingdom, we actually are operating from a feeble, unsteady position. When we draw our power from the world system, of which Lucifer is god, we experience the need to pump ourselves up larger than life—like peacocks.

We become proud. Arrogant. Competitive. We pull others down in order to build ourselves up. We're guilty of exaggerations. Lies. Slander. Gossip. Untrustworthiness. Rejoicing when other people get caught with their pants down. Conniving. Constantly justifying personal behavior. Stirring up strife so that the outward environment matches the internal condition of our hearts.

We are jealous of those who seem to "get away with it." Easily seduced if our ego is massaged. We have no genuine empathy for people who are suffering. We demand time and attention from others and try to make them feel guilty if they don't give it.*

Because Satan's power system is a temporal provision based on guilt, fear and manipulation, we face opposition and pressure without eternal values providing us fortitude. We get smashed into pieces mentally, emotionally, spiritually and, at times, physically. We cave in under the compression of the world, the flesh and the devil.

There is only one way to escape becoming a wolf-

---

* Author's note: Someone suffering from long-standing negative behavior or thought disorders is encouraged to consult a physician. Organic conditions (e.g., a thryroid or glandular problem; salt or sugar imbalance) may contribute to that negative behavior. Such conditions are largely treatable by medication.

like person. We must exercise our personal freedom of choice and begin to incline our hearts toward Jesus. This inclination will also infuse us with wisdom from above when dealing with wolf-like people in our everyday lives.

Remember, we are relative beings. We are the *effect* of which kingdom we relate to, not the *cause* within ourselves. Everything ultimately boils down to a kingdom issue. Choosing to serve life or spiritual death.

When we choose to draw our resources from God's system of authority and power, things are radically different. We are now operating from the position of strength. Merciful toward ourselves and others. Humility that cannot be humiliated. Running without weariness. Walking the second mile without fainting. Willing to admit when wrong. Hospitable without grumbling about the guests behind closed doors. Letting others choose the best. Not saying "I told you so" when our advice has been ignored. Turning the other cheek. Serving without expecting repayment. No defense mechanisms.

Jesus is our pattern and example. The fruit of His life is delicious. He voluntarily came to earth as a vulnerable baby. The demons must have howled in derision. He came to be crucified in weakness. Only someone who operated from a position of strength could risk giving His life for the sake of guilty, ungrateful people. The mystery of God is His patience toward cold, calculated indifference.

He came to die. But you can't keep a resurrected man down! Crucify Him. Stuff Him in a tomb. Roll a 1-1/2 ton rock over its mouth. Post elite Roman guards. Three days later He's alive and well.

You and I are in Christ and His power is available

to us. He is the good Shepherd and we are His sheep. Think about it. He's worth relating to on a consistent basis. And that relation will have a profound positive effect on our behavior.

Points to Ponder

1. Think of a situation where you encountered a person displaying wolf-like behavior. What was your experience like? Did the situation ever get resolved? What is your current attitude toward the other person?

2. Which kingdom are you relating to today?

In Praise of (a Little) Rudeness

To be right with God has often meant to be in trouble with people.
—A. W. Tozer

Do you know someone who lives his life in the "extremes"? Either he is deliriously happy or in the pits of despair. Some days he puts in 16+ hours on the job and other days he won't get out of bed. People he meets are either candidates for sainthood or sinners with a one-way ticket to hell. At times you're his closest friend in the whole world, but some days he treats you like his worst enemy. All gold or all dirt.

It's dangerous living life in extremes. We tend to lose perspective on what's important and what's not. We tend to stereotype everyone we know. We tend to lead a very out-of-balance existence.

Let's take a look at two predominant groupings of believers in the world today who represent the extremes of *Christian* behavior: the S.A.C. (Sloppy Agape Club) and the S.T.C. (Standardized Testing Corps).

To be a member of the S.A.C., one must lack discernment, exhibit great prowess in the realm of spiritual gullibility and diligently avoid conflict at all costs.

An S.A.C. member can be overheard saying, "I just *love* everybody. My rule of thumb is that everybody is good. I'm nice to everyone I know."

I think you know the mentality. It is characterized by a semi-incurable optimism about the goodness that beats in the breast of every being. Even though I'm an optimistic person, I'm not enthusiastic about this naive way of thinking.

I am fascinated by Dr. M. Scott Peck's book, *People of the Lie: The Hope for Healing Human Evil.* While I do not agree with all the theological constructs he has set up, he has opened a can of worms and dumped it in the field of modern psychology. And I say, "Bravo!"

An article appeared in the *Baltimore Sun* when the book was released. Scott made some comments that are worth repeating:

> Over the years in my practice I've had a number of experiences with people who have gone beyond being ordinary sinners—which we all are—to where the sinning seems to be irrevocable, to where they are uncorrectable as people, to where they become more and more fixed in their destructiveness.
>
> This book [*People of the Lie*] grew out of a terrible sense of frustration and helplessness of how to combat or help or heal the damage these people do.
>
> I've come to the conclusion that the disease they're

suffering from is that they're evil. In our profession there's a reluctance to call them that. But I don't see how we're going to be able to heal a disease that we're not willing to study or name.[1]

Dr. Peck says that he usually encounters evil people by being asked to treat their victims. A member of S.A.C. would not take kindly to Peck's assessment of the evil potential of human nature.

At the opposite extreme we'd find a bunch called the S.T.C. (Standardized Testing Corps). This group boasts of members who actually kick wounded Christians and bury them alive. To be a part of this elite crew, one must talk right, dress right, look right and smell right. But above all, one must possess the innate ability to snoop about in other people's business.

The Pharisees of old are perfect examples of an S.T.C. Jesus was drawn to alcoholics, prostitutes and tax collectors. They were people with needs who knew beyond a shadow of a doubt that they were needy. The Pharisees, on the other hand, were hypocritical men who majored on minors and legalistically oppressed the people. They were self-righteous and fixated with externalism—the need to look good. Jesus called these men serpents, vipers and blind guides.

Once when Jesus was talking with a bunch of Pharisees, He exposed the kingdom to which they were relating. He said, "You belong to your father, the devil, and you want to carry out your father's desire. He was a murderer from the beginning. When he lies, he speaks his native language, for he is a liar and the father of lies." Hmmm, all this Kingdom Zoology stuff was started by that "snake in the grass," Lucifer.

In the booklet *The Pharisee in Me: Confessions of a Convicted Religionist*, M. R. De Haan II quotes from the

Talmud, a Jewish collection of laws and commentary. He shows that Israel itself was embarrassed by its Pharisees. Let's take a peek at some of the Pharisees as seen through the eyes of their imaginative contemporaries:

First, the Talmud mentioned the "shoulder" Pharisee. He wore his good deeds outwardly for others to see and shouldered the weight of the religious law so that he could get ahead in his world. His attachment to his religion was more a matter of expediency than principle.

The second was the "wait-a-little" Pharisee who begged for time to put off doing what he should have been doing.

Third was the "bleeding" Pharisee. He wanted to show the world around him that he wasn't lusting after women as he passed them on the street. So he would close his eyes as he walked along, only to stumble against a wall and scrape himself.

The fourth kind of sick religionist mentioned by the Talmud was what it called the "painted" Pharisee. He advertised his holiness so that no unclean person would touch and defile him.

Fifth was the "reckoning" Pharisee, who had a habit of saying, "What good thing should I be doing to balance out what I have neglected to do?"

Sixth was the "fearing" Pharisee, whose relationship to God progressed no further than a negative kind of trembling and awe.[2]

The times have changed, but the S.T.C. remains the same—ever vigilant to criticize and condemn, occupied with issues that won't amount to a hill of beans one thousand years from now.

Without firm guidelines, you or I could easily be

seduced into one of the two extremes of behavior: S.A.C. or S.T.C.

Now that we've considered the dangers of the two extremes represented by the S.A.C. and the S.T.C., let's take a look at how a Christian *should* respond when confronted by a wolf, swine or serpent.

A Study in "Rudeness"

There's a familiar verse in 1 Corinthians 13, the famous "Love Chapter." You've heard it before: "Love does not behave itself unseemly." At first blush it is usually thought that Christians who are filled with love will not behave in a rude, impolite or insulting manner. But is it ever okay to be outraged by people who knowingly behave as wolves, serpents or swine? Believe it or not, there are a number of examples of inconsiderate conduct in the Scriptures.

Consider Elijah. He was a rude dude. Take a look at the way he handled the 450 prophets of Baal at the showdown on Mount Carmel. Elijah mocked the false prophets, sarcastically suggesting that maybe their god had gone to the bathroom or had embarked on a long trip. He told them to raise the decibel level of their voices as they cried for fire to fall. They responded by screaming like maniacs and cutting themselves so blood literally spurted all over the place.

If you or I had been bystanders at the scene, we might have said, "Enough, Elijah. Cool your jets. You can do God's work quietly and reverently. You don't have to make a big deal by embarrassing the prophets so thoroughly. Stop being arrogant. When you do God's work, God's way, you can do it without rubbing the enemy's face in the dirt. You don't have to be impertinent in the process."

Both Paul and John the Baptist said and did things that were uncouth or uncultured by the standards of any age. Think about Peter with Ananias and Sapphira, or Moses with Korah. The list goes on and on.

Jesus, Himself, was hard to figure at times. Why did He demean the Syrophenician woman by implying she was a dog? She had traveled many miles to request healing for her daughter. Why was He so rude to her?

Perhaps the most prominent incident of all is when meek and mild Jesus ran into the temple, overthrowing the tables used by the moneychangers. With red face, clenched teeth and bulging veins in His neck, He drove the buyers and sellers out of the house of God. There was no time for an intellectual, philosophical discussion about temple protocol. He was angry. He was passionate. He put hands and feet to His convictions.

The fact is there is a "rude" side to God that we rarely consider. Many of us are too busy worshiping a predictable God we have created in our own image. He is decent, respectable and benign. He doesn't upset the apple cart. He doesn't make waves. And we can control Him.

Perhaps we've failed to notice the clear picture that God has given of His ultimate attitude toward His enemies. Motivated by unadulterated justice and pure mercy, He laughs. Take a look at Psalm 2:4: "He that sitteth in the heavens shall laugh: The Lord shall have them in derision." Or how about Proverbs 1:26? "I also will laugh at your calamity; I will mock when your fear cometh."

It is also shocking to note that you and I will participate in "holy rudeness" in heaven. I don't know the timetable, but when the Babylonian system crumbles to the ground with all the people in it, both Revelation

18:20 and Revelation 19:4-7 claim that we will "be glad and rejoice." A spontaneous party will erupt when judgment strikes the enemies of God and His people. We'll be shouting, "Hallelujah!"

Learning to Love Wisely

I don't fully understand this. I'm certainly not advocating indiscriminate license with regards to rudeness. But I do believe that when we are confronted by the kingdom of darkness, too much politeness from Christians can cause serious damage to our families, churches and government. Sometimes the best defense is an offense. In *Man: The Dwelling Place of God*, the late A. W. Tozer says it well:

> No man is tolerant when it concerns his life or the life of his child, and no one will agree to negotiate over any religious matter he considers vital to his eternal welfare. Imagine Moses agreeing to take part in a panel discussion with Israel over the golden calf; or Elijah engaging in a gentlemanly dialogue with the prophets of Baal. Or try to picture our Lord Jesus Christ seeking a meeting of minds with the Pharisees to iron out differences. . . .
>
> The desire to be liked, even if not respected, is a great weakness in any man's character, and in that of a minister of Jesus Christ it is a weakness wholly inexcusable. The popular image of the man of God as a smiling, congenial, asexual religious mascot whose handshake is always soft and whose head is always bobbing in the perpetual Yes of universal acquiescence is not the image found in the Scriptures of truth. . . .
>
> . . . some things are not negotiable.[3]

The more we learn about the 1 Corinthians 13 brand of love, the more we tend to resist classifying anyone as a fool, a sheep or a wolf. We all have a

natural bent toward a judgmental spirit. After grasping
the consequences of judging, we develop a healthy caution in that area. And so we should. But perhaps we've
misunderstood what 1 Corinthians is trying to teach us.

If "Love does not behave itself unseemly" is not
talking about rudeness or impoliteness, what does it
mean?

The word *unseemly* in the Greek language is *as-
chemon*,[4] which means a "form, a shape or a structure."
From this we derive the English word *scheme*. A literal
translation of that passage of Scripture would be: "Love
does not behave without a scheme," or "Love does not
behave in a shapeless manner."

Jesus framed people in a system—in a scheme. He
categorizes people in much the same manner as a
zoologist. As we have already seen, He warns about
casting our pearls before swine (Matthew 7:6). In Matthew 25:32, goats and sheep are on either side of Christ.
Peter is commanded to feed sheep and lambs in John
21:15. Jesus coaches us to operate as doves (Matthew
10:16).

In the same vein, Paul warns the elders of Ephesus
about wolves entering the flock (Acts 20:29). In Philippians 3:2 Paul also tells the Christians to be wary of
dogs.

Some people are called sheep. Others are referred
to as wolves, foxes and dogs. Some are blind guides,
hypocrites and fools. Others are friends and beloved
disciples.

What 1 Corinthians 13 is saying is this: *Love does
not behave without having the whole scheme of things in
view.*

The Bible clearly instructs us to love, but it also
teaches us how to respond wisely to wrong attitudes.

The same love that fills our hearts also dictates that we must not respond to hypocrites in the same way we would to beloved disciples and friends. Pity the shepherd who makes no distinction between his sheep and the bears, lions and wolves.

Points to Ponder

1. Do you tend toward S.A.C. or S.T.C.? How do you know? What is the danger in leaning toward either group?

2. Are you frequently "too polite" when a little rudeness is in order? Under what circumstances do you feel it's "right to be rude"?

Famous Last Words

It's when you rub elbows with a man that you find out what he has up his sleeve.
—Anonymous

My grandfather left some precious memories. Among the most special were his last words to me.

Gerhard Schroeder lived a full life. He was full of "white knuckle" adventure stories. He served as the Volost secretary for the White Army during the Russian Revolution. The most violent peasant uprisings and bandit raids in the history of the Russian Civil War took place in the Mennonite communities of the Ukraine where he lived. Yet he and my grandmother miraculously survived and were helped financially by the Mennonites. They were able to sail to North America in the early 1920s. Once here, he pastored in Canada and the United States.

Approximately six months before he was promoted to heaven, I paid him a visit at his home in

Lodi, California. For a week, I spent hours every day "priming the pump" and sitting back to listen to his stories about the old country. What a treasured memory!

I can still see the look in his eyes and hear the fervency in his voice on our last afternoon together. Before what was to be our final goodbye, he said, "Joel, never deviate from the Word of God. You must always remain true to this book." While talking, he held his well-worn Bible to his chest for emphasis. His tone was somber. He warned me about some of the pitfalls of the ministry. Much of his advice sprang from his dealings with wicked people. He had suffered much at the hands of individuals both inside and outside the circles of Christianity.

Months after that visit, I embarked on a study of the last recorded words of famous Bible characters. To my surprise, a common thread seemed to weave their final words together into a rather dark, foreboding tapestry. Like my grandfather's counsel, their closing remarks included either direct or indirect warnings about evil people. Two-legged wolves, if you please. It's worth noting.

Last Words of Learned Men

Moses had led the nation of Israel for some forty years. Before he died, he composed a song (see Deuteronomy 32). When Moses finished reciting the words of his song to the nation, he said, "Take to heart all the words that I have solemnly declared to you this day, so that you may command your children to obey carefully all the words of this law. They are not just idle words for you—they are your life. By them you will live long in the land you are crossing the Jordan to possess" (Deuteronomy 32:46,47).

Moses knew that the nation was about to experience a blitzkrieg of temptation in Canaan. At every turn the Israelites would be confronted by enemies of Jehovah who possessed ulterior motives and would seek to destroy the moral fiber of God's chosen people. His inspired song would be there to help keep the people from becoming a nation without direction.

Years later, King David came on the scene. In 2 Samuel 23, David's last words are penned. Notice how this "sweet psalmist" mustered up the strength on his deathbed to take a parting shot at ungodly men: "The sons of Belial shall be all of them as thorns thrust away, because they cannot be taken with hands" (2 Samuel 23:6).

To whom was David referring? I don't know. But the significant thing is that David was compelled to mention the sons of Belial at such a tender moment. His harsh words were nestled in the midst of glowing statements about his three mighty men and about God, the Rock of Israel. His words had a note of caution about them.

A leap forward in time brings us to the apostle Paul. I imagine Paul to be like a five-foot bantam rooster, always stirring up trouble. He couldn't even take an off-duty walk in a strange city like Athens without causing a riot. Yet the people he taught held a deep love and respect for him. They looked beneath the seemingly caustic exterior and could see a warm, sensitive guy underneath.

Acts 20 portrays a touching event. Paul has sent for the elders from Ephesus, gathering them together for some last words:

> I know that after I leave, savage wolves will come in among you and will not spare the flock. Even from your

own number men will arise and distort the truth in order
to draw away disciples after them. So be on your guard!
Remember that for three years I never stopped warning
each of you night and day with tears (Acts 20:29-31, NIV).

When Paul finished his remarks, they all wept
profusely as they embraced and kissed him. A study of
the history of the Ephesian church verifies that Paul's
warning about wolves was prophetic.

Later, around A.D. 66, during his second imprison-
ment in Rome, Paul wrote 2 Timothy. This was the last
epistle written before his martyrdom. The book is
chock-full of warnings about heretical doctrines and
counterfeit teachers. He names names: Phygellus, Her-
mogenes, Hymenaeus and Philetus. When Paul said,
"Beware of dogs," is it possible that some of these men
were on his mind?

Obviously, encounters with evil men were of
enough importance to several men of God to warrant
attention to the subject in their parting words. Perhaps
we would do well to heed their final warnings.

Jesus also warned His disciples that a time would
come when anyone who killed them would think he
was offering a service to God. Persecution from evil
men was part of the package when they signed up to be
His disciples. They lived in a demanding hour of
human history, as we shall see in the next chapter.

Points to Ponder

1. Do you tend to heed warnings or ignore them?
   Are you usually satisfied with the outcome?

2. If you knew you had twenty-four hours left to
   live, what would be the primary thing you would
   want to communicate to your loved ones? Would
   there be any words of caution?

Malice in Wonderland

Truth is incontrovertible. Panic may resent it; ignorance may deride it; malice may distort it; but there it is.
—Winston Churchill

Remember *Alice in Wonderland?* Alice was the rather bored little girl sitting on a riverbank one hot summer day. Suddenly a white rabbit with pink eyes ran close by her muttering, "Oh dear! Oh dear! I shall be late!" He took a watch out of his waistcoat pocket and looked at it.

The entire scene was too curious for her. In a flash, Alice followed the white rabbit down a large rabbit hole under a hedge and started the descent into the brilliantly nonsensical place called Wonderland. Before she awoke from her dream, she had met such delightful creatures as the Mad Hatter, the Cheshire Cat, Mock Turtle and the Caterpillar.

I get the feeling that the first-century church was a

kind of "Wonderland" filled with fascinating characters. I don't know if there were any Mad Hatters, but
imagine what it would have been like to travel with
Paul or to engage in a lively discussion about spiritual
discernment with Peter. Do you ever wish you could
have lived during that time? I do!

There is a big part of me that thrives on romance
and adventure. I think it would be exciting to jump in a
time machine and travel back to the days of the early
church. If I had my way, I'd program that machine to
land among a small group of bathrobed people who are
straining to hear every word from a wizened old
apostle by the name of John. John has a lot to say about
how to be alert for the wolves in sheep's clothing.

John's Assessment of the Early Church

Before John died (around A.D. 100), he had the opportunity to observe the spiritual condition of at least
three generations of Christians since the time of Christ.
It was a thrilling hour of human history. Churches were
planted all over the known world during this period.
Ancient forms of paganism were challenged by an
empty tomb. Lives were transformed by the power of
God.

At the same time, however, John could discern
some fundamental problems with the new church.
Several factors complicated its growth. For starters,
Nero, the neurotic, out-of-touch-with-reality Emperor
of Rome, had initiated the brutal persecution of those
who named Christ as Lord and Savior (around A.D. 64).
As the brutality intensified, the Christians placed
greater hope in the promised return of Jesus to spare
them from their troubles. After all, He had said He'd
come again to snatch them out of their trials and
tribulations.

With external persecution came internal strife. The Christians had long since gone underground—literally, in some cases. It cost a lot to be counted as a disciple. Many were giving up hope. Was the imminent return of Christ a lie? Was the resurrection of Jesus a big hoax? Did God really care? Was He listening to their pleas? Was the supposed glory of heaven worth all the suffering?

At the local level, every gathering of believers fought a battle against heresy. What was truth? By what final authority was that truth to be determined? Could all the ancient pagan religions that the masses followed be wrong? What human being could claim that he had the only pipeline to eternal truth, anyway?

What made matters even more complicated was the myriad of prophets who wandered about the countryside, going from church to church and preaching their own pet doctrines. There were false ones and true ones. But who could tell the difference?

Sophisticated Evil

Wandering prophets enjoyed enormous prestige. Many homes, in fact, had a chamber especially reserved for these men. The local inns were notoriously dirty and flea-infested. The philosopher Plato compared innkeepers to pirates who held their guests for ransom before they allowed them to escape. In contrast, the Christian climate was one of unconditional love and open-armed hospitality. Or, in some cases, gullibility.

You can easily see how attractive this arrangement would be for certain wolf-type, swine-type people. "Oh yeah, I'll be a prophet," they begin. "Give me a few acting lessons and I'll be able to switch from tears to righteous indignation in an Athenian second! Where do I sign up?"

Even the pagan satirists recognized the problem. One Greek writer, Lucian, penned *Peregrinus*, a story about a man who discovered a way to live off the fat of the land without raising one bead of sweat. As an itinerant charlatan, he cruised from church to church, enjoying luxury at others' expense.

Unfortunately, this was happening all too often in the early Christian church. An undesirable character could set himself up as a prophet. He could spiritually, emotionally and financially "rape" a local body of believers and could be gone before the church knew what had hit them. Without telephones, fax machines or telegrams, it was relatively easy for that man to then sting a group in the neighboring city. He could live a pampered life for years without repercussions.

Guidelines to Detecting the Phony Sheep

Still in its infant stages of growth, the church was not equipped to handle such sophisticated forms of evil. Around A.D. 100, in an attempt to tackle the problems at hand, the early church fathers began laying down definite regulations to address the dangers. *The Didachē* was the result of their effort. Note the specific yet balanced nature with which they took aim at these teachers with knapsacks:

> Whosoever, therefore, shall come and teach you all these things aforesaid, receive him. But if the teacher himself turn and teach another doctrine to pervert, hear him not. . . . Let every apostle that cometh unto you be received as the Lord. And he shall stay one day, and if need be, the next also, but, if he stay three, he is a false prophet. And when the apostle goeth forth, let him take nothing save bread, till he reach his lodging, but, if he ask money, he is a false prophet. . . . And every prophet that teacheth the truth, if he doeth not what he teacheth,

is a false prophet. . . . Whosoever shall say in the Spirit: Give me money, or any other thing, ye shall not hearken unto him: but if he bid you give for others who are in need, let no man judge him.

Let everyone that cometh in the name of the Lord be received. . . . But, if he be minded to settle among you, and be a craftsman, let him work and eat. . . . But if he will not do this, he is a Christmonger: of such men beware.[1]

Try to imagine the scene. A visiting prophet stands up in a fully packed house meeting. He strokes his beard thoughtfully with eyes darting to and fro. Everyone is looking in his direction, waiting for his words of wisdom. He shuts his eyelids tightly and begins to groan softly. He must be experiencing the anointing of the Spirit.

He stops, opens his eyes and gives a piercing glance to everyone in the room. "Bow your heads, everyone," he begins. "The Spirit of the Lord has given me a word. I must obey Him. He has instructed me to tell you that there are six, no wait, seven people present in this room who are to give fifty denarii for my ministry. Ooooo yes, I can sense His presence." His voice begins to rise with emotion. "You know who you are. Respond now with an upraised hand and the Lord will bless you with abundant prosperity."

A hush falls on the room. No one moves. The prophet continues to scan the congregation. Without a flourish, an older man rises to his feet.

"Sir," he begins tactfully as every head in the place jerks to attention, "you have been with us for a few weeks, and I have enjoyed you up till now. Two days ago I received a copy of *The Didachē* and have been studying it carefully. According to this manuscript, you are a phony. Not only have you stayed in our community longer than two days without working, but now you are asking for money for yourself under the supposed influence of the Holy Spirit. We can no longer accept this form of deceit."

This type of situation was probably repeated many times during the first century.

And John wasn't the only one concerned with the spiritual well-being of the church. Jude hastily wrote the epistle which some current scholars deem to be the most relevant book in the New Testament. Those power-packed verses contain warnings about men who had secretly slipped in among the rank and file. These men had the appearance of godliness. Reality was different. They actually were engaged in changing the grace of God into a license for flagrant, Sodom and Gomorrah-type immorality. And since a man's morality tends to dictate his theology, their teachings were cleverly designed to deny the deity of Christ and the reliability of God's Word.

These perverse men were likened to Balaam, Cain and Korah. A casual study of those three examples will send shivers up and down your spine. Jude then provided principles to assist us in remaining strong and clear-headed under the increasing pressure of apostasy:

1. Build your life on the foundation of the most holy faith.

2. Be a person of prayer with desires purified by the Holy Spirit.

3. Keep in the love of God.

4. Maintain an expectant hope regarding the coming of Jesus.

5. Be ready to defend the faith by studying and then speaking up for the truth.

6. Be ready to forcibly snatch some people from hell-fire and damnation.

7. Rescue troubled people. Love the sinner, but hate the sin.

8. Remember that God is able to keep us from slipping.

9. God can make us stand blameless in the presence of His glory.

10. We can enter into His presence with joyous certainty.

11. The love of God is at once our present atmosphere and future goal.

The apostle Peter was a contemporary of both John and Jude. Peter's two books help to sharpen the focus of the discerning eye. He brought everything back to the objectivity of the Scriptures. All experience, whether ecstatic or mundane, must be tested by the Book. All teachings must be subservient to God's Word.

I get the feeling that we could be talking about the twentieth-century church here. Everything seems to be changing, yet nothing changes. Like King Solomon said, "There's nothing new under the sun." While we may not have a false prophet asking for our money, secularism, modernism, humanism and much more are invading the church of Christ today with just as many lies. Along with all the wonderful blessings from Almighty God come the wiles of our enemy, Satan.

If John, Jude or Peter were still alive and facing the challenges we face today, they would be playing the same tune from the same sheet of music. Nothing changes, especially counsel from the Book that has stood the test of time.

It would have been wonderful to have lived during the age of the apostles. In many ways, it would have been like a Wonderland minus the Mad Hatter. But in the midst of it all, there was still much malice poured out from the pits of hell.

Points to Ponder

1. The first-century church faced many challenges. What do you think are the top three challenges facing the church today? How does Scripture address these problems?

2. Is it harder to live for Jesus in this modern era? Why or why not?

Legend in My Own Mind

*Our greatest pretenses are built up not to hide the
evil and the ugly in us, but our emptiness.
The hardest thing to hide is something
that is not there.*
—Eric Hoffer

If I seem to be striking a cautionary note thus far, it's partly because of personal experience. You see, I have played the part of a self-centered fool—a wolf in training. My precious parents have endured much heartache from my beast-like behavior. Take a step back with me.

As a rebellious teenager, I absolutely despised my father. With my older brother, Dad had tried the "Mr. Tough-Guy" approach. Steve left home in the tenth grade. Thinking he had gone overboard with Steve in terms of discipline, Dad went to the opposite extreme and tried the "Mr. Nice-Guy" approach with me. I walked all over him and ultimately left home at the world-owes-me-a-living age of seventeen. I was becoming a S.P.A.S.M. child—Simply Pray And Send Money.

I can remember the day before I left my Canadian home. I found myself contemptuously slouched in the doorway of my bedroom with my hands stuffed deeply in my pockets.

Like hair on a gorilla, my father was all over me about something I had done. I can't recall the exact reason for our confrontation. All I can remember is the utter disdain I felt for him. He was baffled and I was like a brick wall.

My dad didn't realize it, but one of my best friends, Bob, and I had been plotting to leave home for some time. This encounter had pushed me over the edge.

I glared at him coldly. "I hate you and everything you stand for," I pronounced. "I hate your God and your religion. I'm leaving home. I'm gone."

The last thing my father said to me was, "Son, when you get hungry, you'll be home." That statement made me even more determined to make it on my own. I stubbornly set my course.

What a sight Bob and I were the next day! Two young punks with loaded backpacks stepping out in the sub-zero Albertan temperature. Dad and Mom must have been in agony. With $24 in my pocket, I stuck out my thumb. Free at last!

I was intoxicated with my new-found liberty. No restraints. Nobody to tell me what to do or when to do it. If I got bored with one place there was a simple solution: Just stick out the thumb and move on. It was life on the edge. Never a dull moment. A rebel without a pause.

The reality was that I was living for myself. No one else really mattered. I was a legend in my own mind. A wolf in training. A fool.

Oh, sure, I had pangs of guilt every once in a while. I knew I was building personal happiness on the heartache of others, especially my parents. There was even the occasional night that I'd get teary-eyed after a telephone call or letter from my parents.

I knew they were praying for me. I hated that.

The Prodigal Finds His Way Home

On September 10, 1972, I changed. I accepted Jesus Christ as my personal Savior and entered Bible school the very next day. It was wonderful.

The relationship with my father and mother definitely improved from that point on, but was still strained. Approximately one year after my conversion, the Holy Spirit convicted me of the need to repent to my parents for all the harm I had caused them.

I called long distance from New England to Alberta, Canada. My mother answered the phone and immediately lit up at the sound of my voice. "Arthur," I could hear her call, "it's Joel. Hurry, get on the other phone."

In a matter of seconds, both of them were on the line. "Dad, Mom," I began tentatively, "I have something to say that should have been said a long time ago. I called to tell you both how sorry I am for all the pain I caused you when I left home. Please forgive me."

All was quiet on the other end of the line. Then I could hear some sniffling. They were crying. "Of course, we forgive you," they responded.

I had been trying to do this without losing control, but my tears were close to the surface. My mom and dad then asked me to forgive them for not being perfect parents. That's when I lost it.

If you could see me at my writing desk today, penning these words, you'd probably wonder why I was grinning from ear to ear. You see, I love my father and mother. I am grateful that we were able to reconcile while there was still time. I am also thankful that our fellowship has grown sweeter as the years have passed.

The Key to Detecting a Fool

When we play the part of the fool, we don't always have the luxury of seeing God's grace repair the damage. Each of us has reaped bountiful crops that have been the result of personal foolishness. Believe me, I speak with authority here. We also deal on a continual basis with fools. It is, therefore, vital to our spiritual growth that we gain a biblical frame of reference regarding the subject of fools. If we can properly discern foolishness, we can confront it in our lives as well as in the lives of others within our sphere of influence.

What do you think is the trademark of a fool? How can you spot foolishness a mile off? The footnote to Proverbs 14:3 in the Amplified Bible offers some interesting insight:

> The word "fool" in the Old Testament seldom, if ever, means feebleminded, imbecile, idiot, or moron. Rather, it always has in it the meaning of rebel, especially against God and the laws of order, decency, and justice.[1]

Rebellion is the key to detecting the fool. The word *rebel* in the Hebrew language has various meanings, some of which are: to be bitter, to resist, to be disobedient, to provoke, to break away from just authority, to trespass, to apostatize, to quarrel, to offend and to revolt.[2]

Whew, that's a lot to think about! The fact is that when we rebel against specific mandates in Scripture, we actually are expressing hatred toward God. And if we continue, we will ultimately mount an offensive, organized attack against God. Rebellion cannot remain passive.

As the author of rebellion, Satan's main goal is to dull the hearts of people so that they will make choices that relate to his kingdom. Soon they are drawn into believing and making decisions based on foolish, vain philosophies (e.g., There is no heaven or hell; If someone hurts you, get revenge; Live for comfort, convenience and personal pleasure.).

The average Christian recoils at the mere thought of being deceived by the Satanic kingdom and playing the part of a fool. Unfortunately, it's true that many Christians hold fast to an orthodox theological statement, but continually, habitually and repeatedly relate to the kingdom of darkness. They exhibit wolf-type, swine-type behavior in their gossip, slander, unethical business practices, cliquishness, retaliation and argumentativeness.

God gives precise definitions of wrong character based on the Hebrew words for *simple, mocker, scorner, fool* and *folly*. Five categories of fools are mentioned in the Old Testament:

1. Simple Fool—*pethîy*

2. Unreasonable Fool—*evîyl*

3. Stubborn Fool—*kecîyl*

4. Mocking Fool—*lûwts*

5. Committed Fool—*nâbâl*

Don your Sherlock Holmes hat. Carefully polish your magnifying glass. We're on our way to the book of Proverbs. As we embark upon the discovery of five types of fools, be prepared to learn how to detect foolishness and then understand the biblical responses to each of these wrong attitudes. The five types of fools are a fundamental part of learning to deal with the wolves, serpents and swine in your life.

Anyone can play the part of a fool, nice church-going people included.

Points to Ponder

1. Think about some "wolfish" scenes from your own past. Have you dealt with them scripturally? If not, do you feel that rebellious qualities are keeping a foothold in your life?

2. How does your definition of "fool" differ from how it's used in the Old Testament? Keep this in mind as you study the next few chapters.

Sheepish in Wolf Country

Men and nations can only be reformed in their youth; they become incorrigible as they grow old.
—*Rousseau*

P. T. Barnum said it best: "There's a sucker born every minute."

We all chuckle somewhat nervously when we meet a person who is easily fooled. You know the type. He falls for lines like, "Wanna buy the Brooklyn Bridge?" Or "I've got some swampland in Florida to sell you." Or "You can make a million bucks with no work and no money down!"

Now pause for a moment and reflect on your life. As you sift through the memories, search for and focus on the moments you were gullible, easily deceived, inexperienced, overtrusting, an accident looking for a place to happen.

Perhaps you lost your shirt on a get-rich-quick scheme. Or maybe you gave large donations to a non-profit organization only to discover later that the whole operation was fraudulent. You should have known better. Or perhaps you fell in love with someone. You look back at the relationship now with chagrin, realizing that you gave emotionally, sexually and financially while your partner took advantage of you.

Slowly but surely the truth of your situation dawned on you. No mistake about it—you were gullible. What was your emotional state after unraveling the sordid details? Shock? Denial? Anger? Embarrassment? Bitterness? Resignation?

We live in a dog-eat-dog society. There are all kinds of scams perpetrated by wolves who prey on uninitiated simple folk. It's wrong. It's unjust. But we're living in "Wolf Country."

This type of foolishness is best described by the word, *simple*. *Pethîy*,[1] the Hebrew equivalent, literally means to be open, unguarded in a mental and moral sense. It represents people who are easily persuaded by flattery, delusion, deception and/or enticement. These people are inexperienced and quickly awed by the allurement of the world. Newborn or immature Christians are especially susceptible.

You may be thinking, *Hey, that's not me. I'm not an easy mark.* Sure, we all have areas of strength. But they are joined by areas of potential weakness. Think about the take-no-prisoners businessman who thrives successfully in unpredictable economic matters because of his market prowess. He's no dummy. Yet after hours, his personal life is in shambles. His weakness for beautiful women (matched by an enormous ego) keeps him floundering from one sexually-charged encounter to the next. Without a doubt, he's a fool.

In each chapter on "fools," we'll take a look at some verses that use the Hebrew word we're studying and briefly comment on how the Scriptures apply to us today. Get ready! We're in for some hard-hitting lessons about the fool in all of us.

How to Detect Simple Foolishness

• **Proverbs 22:3**   A prudent man foresees evil and hides himself, but the *simple* pass on and are punished.

When simple fools are not filled with specific instruction from the Word, they lack foresight and caution with regard to spiritual danger. They haven't been trained. Unfortunately, the catch for most of us is that we know too much and follow too little.

• **Proverbs 7:7-27**   Once I was looking out the window of my house, and I saw many *inexperienced* young men, but noticed one *foolish* fellow in particular. He was walking along the street near the corner where a certain woman lived. He was passing near her house in the evening after it was dark. And then she met him; she was dressed like a prostitute and was making plans. . . . She threw her arms around the young man, kissed him, looked him straight in the eye, and said, " . . . I wanted to find you and here you are! . . . Come on! Let's make love all night long. We'll be happy in each other's arms. My husband isn't at home. He's on a long trip . . . ." So she tempted him with her charms, and he gave in to her smooth talk. Suddenly he was going with her like an ox on the way to be slaughtered, like a deer prancing into a trap where an arrow would pierce its heart. He

was like a bird going into a net—he did
not know that his life was in danger.

Now then, sons, listen to me. Pay attention to what I say. Do not let such a
woman win your heart; don't go
wandering after her. She has been the
ruin of many men and caused the
death of too many to count. If you go to
her house, you are on the way to the
world of death. It is a shortcut to death
(TEV).

Flattery will score points with an empty-hearted,
empty-headed individual. Simple fools are easily
seduced by smooth-talking members of the opposite
sex who inflate their egos by reassuring them of their
desirability. When all is said and done, though, both
parties feel used and disillusioned because of seeking
satisfaction from the wrong source.

Simple fools lack the discernment that is needed
when coming up against people who try to justify their
loose morality.

- **Proverbs 14:15**   A *simple* man believes anything, but a
                        prudent man gives thought to his steps
                        (NIV).

Simple fools are ready to believe almost anything
if given even the slightest evidence. They exhibit great
gullibility for gossip, slander, false teaching and get-
rich-quick schemes.

- **Proverbs 1:22**   *Foolish* people! How long do you want
                       to be *foolish*? How long will you enjoy
                       making fun of knowledge? Will you
                       ever learn? (TEV)

Since simple fools are thoughtless in a spiritual

sense, and since it is the only lifestyle they know, they love being simple. To them, planned ignorance is bliss.

How Simple Foolishness Is Treated

- **Psalm 19:7b**   The testimony of the Lord is sure, making wise the *simple*.

- **Psalm 119:130**   The entrance of your words gives light; it gives understanding to the *simple* (NIV).

- **Proverbs 1:4**   Here are proverbs . . . They can make an *inexperienced* person clever and teach young men how to be resourceful (TEV).

- **Proverbs 8:5a**   O y o u *simple* ones, understand prudence.

The entire first chapter of Proverbs is dedicated to the importance and positive results of teaching simple fools. Simple fools must take a crash course in information from Scripture on key subjects. The Word of God will begin to correct their souls, thus giving them much-needed foresight, discernment and unwavering convictions. They are to be taught with firmness and compassion.

For the most part, simple fools are led by their emotions. Only the Word, understood in the power of the Holy Spirit, can provide the necessary objectivity required to function with wisdom.

- **Proverbs 19:25**   Flog [discipline] a mocker, and the *simple* will learn prudence; rebuke a discerning man, and he will gain knowledge (NIV).

- **Proverbs 21:11**   When the scoffer is punished, the *simple* is made wise; but when the wise is instructed, he receives knowledge.

Another form of help for the simple fool involves precise discipline by a church or a family. These two verses point out that simple fools learn prudence when viewing the punishment of mocking fools (we will discuss them later). Because of the positive effects of loving discipline upon simple fools, I'd like to touch on this controversial subject now.

Within the church of Jesus Christ, discipline is almost non-existent. Its demise can mostly be attributed to lax standards, sentimentality and fear. Basically, two things are feared:

1. what the deacons, elders, church members and community might do;

2. a law suit.

Yet if a church leader is persistently teaching heresy, if there are irresolvable disputes between people, if a swindler sets up shop in the congregation, if someone is committed to an immoral lifestyle, loving discipline is vital.

Most of us have heard or observed "horror stories" about church discipline. I believe that 99 percent of all cases can be handled quietly and behind closed doors if the offending person is approached in genuine humility, meekness and tears. I've found that most people will respond positively if they sense love and authentic concern.

I'm a firm believer, though, in allowing the offending party to choose the forum. If he or she chooses to raise a big stink, then the matter must be dealt with in a public fashion, but in a most gracious and non-accusatory manner. If it is a private concern, no one else, not even a close associate, has to know. Taking this approach honors God and leaves the responsibility of choice with the individual. Redemptive discipline is interested in restoration, not exposition.

- **Proverbs 27:12**   A prudent man foresees evil and hides himself; the *simple* pass on and are punished.

If simple fools reject repeated instructions and warnings from the Scriptures, they will encounter great personal distress. They reap self-inflicted wounds because they sow according to the urgent desires of their flesh. They do not foresee danger and thereby suffer accordingly. And if they're not careful, will acquire the lifestyle of the unreasonable fool.

Summary

Every person alive has experienced this category of foolishness, whether in himself or others. When we encounter the simple fool, we can try to help the person by pointing out the ultimate end of sin. In the Bible, God gives us an unvarnished view of His saints—warts and all. We can read about a believer who blew it, and then we can glean wisdom from his mistakes. We don't have to be personally burned by evil in order to hate it.

Any time we ignore prudent instruction, we are behaving foolishly.

Points to Ponder

1. The last time you felt you'd acted foolishly, was it because you were ignorant of biblical principles or too stubborn to follow them? What steps can you take to head off the next "wolf" at the pass?

2. Have you ever exhibited any of the characteristics of a simple fool? If so, what changes can be made in your life?

Heifers Without a Cause

Some people will pay their tuition, and then
defy you to give them an education.
—Robert A. Cook

It was the summer of '69. A busy time for newspaper reporters in America:

Woodstock Festival: A Coming Together for Rock,
Drugs, Sex and Peace

Neil Armstrong on the Moon: "The Eagle Has Landed"

Kennedy Drives Off Chappaquiddick Bridge,
Kopechne Drowns

Nixon Orders 25,000 Troops Out of Viet Nam

Tate Murdered by Manson Cult Group

Judy Garland Finds End of Rainbow

But I remember the summer of '69 for other reasons. My parents had arranged for me to spend the few months of vacation working on a dairy farm in Litchfield, Maine. The owners were long-time family friends. It was the very first time I had ever spent more than an at-camp week away from home. And I was excited.

My responsibilities included helping at the 4 A.M. and 4 P.M. milkings, mowing and baling hay, painting the house, keeping the garden free of weeds and seeing to a host of other odd jobs. Hunting for woodchucks, fishing, horseback riding or just plain hanging around filled what little free time was left. It was a well-rounded experience.

One particularly hot, sweaty day in July, my boss Fred backed the truck into the barnyard and we attempted the impossible—loading heifers to take to market.

Heifers are young, full-of-spit-and-vinegar female cows that have not yet calved. They are nervous creatures that telegraph a half-crazed look if you get too close to them. They snort, run a short distance and then stop and watch your every move with a vacant kind of stare. You're not sure if they want to charge you, kick you or run in the opposite direction. All three options are exasperating if you're trying to catch them in a large pasture on a sweltering day.

It was tedious. One of us would pull on the rope attached to the halter while the other prodded from the rear with a stick. After much bellowing and snorting, the heifers were pushed one by one up the ramp and on to the truck. Off they went to market.

Many years have passed, but the memory of my brief encounter with heifers has not diminished. It certainly brings into sharp focus Jehovah's view of the nation of Israel in their backslidden, "let's-do-what-we-want-to-when-we-want-to" condition. In the book of Hosea, God called them a herd of heifers.

That assessment fit them perfectly. They behaved

like spoiled brats. In fact, our second category of foolishness describes them well.

The Hebrew word for the heifer-like unreasonable fool is *evîyl*.[1] This term describes one who is without aim or counsel. It is talking about the person who is ready to commit everything to an uncertain cause. The real problems gurgle to the surface when this type of fool brashly opposes those who desire to walk in obedience to the Scriptures. Christians behave like heifers sometimes.

How to Detect Unreasonable Foolishness

- **Proverbs 1:7**   *Fools* despise wisdom and instruction.
- **Proverbs 10:21**   *Fools* die for lack of judgment.
- **Proverbs 15:14**   The heart of him that hath understanding seeketh knowledge: but the mouth of *fools* feedeth on *foolishness*.
- **Proverbs 24:7**   Wisdom is too high for a *fool*; in the assembly at the gate he has nothing to say (NIV).

With arrogance, unreasonable fools despise wisdom and instruction. People who reject godly wisdom are left with an empty shell—themselves. This type of fool tends to condemn the talents of others, point out the faults in others and disdain acts of kindness from those around him. It is the kind of contempt calculated to provoke anger in others.

- **Proverbs 22:15**   *Foolishness* is bound in the heart of a child; but the rod of correction shall drive it far from him.

Children are born with the idea that the universe revolves around them. Unreasonable foolishness is firmly fixed in the heart of every child. Parents know that if they cater to every whim during the early years, they will pay a dear price later on. A tiny spoiled brat soon becomes a giant spoiled monster whose unreasonable demands are backed up by muscle, malice and mouth.

- **Proverbs 14:3**   A *fool's* talk brings a rod to his back (NIV).

- **Proverbs 17:28**   Even a *fool* is thought wise if he keeps silent, and discerning if he holds his tongue (NIV).

- **Proverbs 18:13**   He who answers before listening—that is his *folly* and his shame (NIV).

Unreasonable fools are easy to spot. They suffer from brain-in-neutral-mouth-in-gear syndrome. Self-conceit betrays them as they give answers before the whole matter is heard. The only time unreasonable fools appear wise is when their mouths are shut.

- **Proverbs 5:23**   He shall die without instruction; and in the greatness of his *folly* he shall go astray.

- **Proverbs 20:3**   It is to a man's honor to avoid strife, but every *fool* is quick to quarrel (NIV).

- **Proverbs 29:9**   If a wise man contendeth with a *foolish* man, whether he rage or laugh, there is no rest.

All efforts to pacify an unreasonable fool, whether severe or gentle, seem to be of no avail. He lacks self-discipline and control and is habitually unsettled in his lifestyle.

- **Proverbs 27:3**   A stone is heavy, and the sand weighty; but a *fool's* wrath is heavier than them both.

Unreasonable fools have illogical and excessive anger. It is hard to know what to say, how to say it or when to communicate sensitive subject matter to them. In fact, it seems like there is never a good time to do so.

* **Proverbs 14:9**   *Fools* mock at making amends for sin (NIV).
* **Proverbs 27:22**   Though you grind a *fool* in a mortar, grinding him like grain with a pestle, you will not remove his *folly* from him (NIV).

Sin has three stages:

1. Pleasure Stage. Much fun and excitement. No consequences in view.

2. Bondage Stage. Imprisoned by sin's addiction. Denial of reality.

3. Sickening Stage. Bitter results taking their toll. Robbed of hope.

Although continually wandering into sin's trap, unreasonable fools belittle its dangers. Consequently, they are consistently enticed and allured by its pleasures. Even the heaviest affliction doesn't seem to penetrate their pattern of foolishness as they obstinately walk down the path of evil desires.

How Unreasonable Foolishness Is Treated

* **Proverbs 22:15**   *Folly* is bound up in the heart of a child, but the rod of discipline will drive it far from him (NIV).

Dr. James Dobson delineates the difference between *discipline* and *punishment*. In essence, he says that *discipline* meted out by a parent is for the positive benefit of shaping the child's will while preserving the child's spirit. *Punishment*, on the other hand, is for the benefit of the parent—releasing anger, frustration and harsh words at the child's expense. In *Dr. Dobson Answers Your Questions*, he outlines six broad guidelines that represent his philosophy of discipline:[2]

1. Define the boundaries before enforcing them.

2. When defiantly challenged, respond with confident decisiveness.

3. Distinguish between willful defiance and childish irresponsibility.

4. Reassure and teach after the confrontation is over.

5. Avoid impossible demands.

6. Let love be your guide.

In an effort to keep our children safe from the deceptions of Satan, we must define and enforce certain limits. Actually, our children are begging for well-grounded guidelines. In time, genuine convictions will replace enforced discipline. This is vital for our kids' success in the adult world.

- **Psalm 107:17**   Some became *fools* through their rebellious ways and suffered affliction because of their iniquities (NIV).

- **Proverbs 10:8**   The wise in heart accept commands, but a chattering *fool* comes to ruin (NIV).

If you plant corn seeds, you expect to harvest ears of corn a few months later. If an unreasonable fool plants rebellion, anger or empty-headed conversation, sooner or later it will come back to him as a crop of heartache and pain. God is not mocked.

Summary

Unreasonable foolishness is present in our lives from the day we were born. If we lovingly deal with this type of foolishness when our children are young, they will have a better chance of growing into non-foolish adults. Young children are like unformed lumps of clay crying out for the potter's touch. You can bet that Satan will take advantage of our kids at every turn, cleverly enticing them into progressively darker forms of evil. Be ready to deal with the unreasonable fool in your midst.

Points to Ponder

1. Have you ever seen evidences of the unreasonable fool in your own life? If so, what can you do to change that?

2. How would you handle a friend, co-worker or family member who exhibits this brand of foolishness?

3. If you are a parent, what three principles from this chapter can you apply to your child-raising skills?

South End of a North-Bound Mule

A troublemaker is a guy who rocks the boat, then persuades everyone else there is a storm at sea.
—Anonymous

The unspectacular offspring of a jackass and a female horse is the mule, beast of burden. Despite the bad press mules have gotten, their strength, stamina, intelligence and size make them excellent pack animals. Most mules are not high-strung and will accept hard work, poor handling and maltreatment without a whimper.

But every once in a while, you meet a brute with fire in his eyes, one who lives up to the reputation "stubborn as a mule." And no matter how hard you beat the south end of these passive-aggressive creatures, they remain unconquerable, indomitable. They will hunker down, look the other way and endure any abuse you throw their way.

This mule-headed manner reminds me of the third classification of fools. *Kecîyl*[1] is the Hebrew word used when referring to the stubborn brand of foolishness. This Old Testament term paints a picture of an extremely fat person. His loins and flanks are so crowded that he can barely move. What motion he can muster is dull and lethargic. Spiritually speaking, the stubborn fool has obstinately set his rebellious heart and is not moved by godly reason or counsel. Christians are not exempt from this brand of foolishness.

How to Detect Stubborn Foolishness

- **Proverbs 10:1**   A wise son makes a glad father, but a *foolish* son is the grief of his mother.
- **Proverbs 15:20**   A *foolish* man despises his mother (NIV).
- **Proverbs 17:21**   The father of a *fool* has no joy.
- **Proverbs 17:25**   A *foolish* son brings grief to his father and bitterness to the one who bore him (NIV).
- **Proverbs 19:13**   A *foolish* son is the ruin of his father (NIV).

Stubborn fools produce grief and anguish for their parents. They absolutely despise their parents and take advantage of every opportunity to shame them. They break their parents' hearts with a most painful sorrow.

These fools cannot cope with legitimate authority in business or in the church for any great length of time. This is especially true if the one in authority asks a stubborn fool to perform a task that somehow inconveniences him.

- **Proverbs 10:18**   He who conceals his hatred has lying lips, and whoever spreads slander is a *fool* (NIV).
- **Proverbs 12:23**   The heart of *fools* proclaim *foolishness*.

- **Proverbs 15:14**   The discerning heart seeks knowledge, but the mouth of a *fool* feeds on *folly* (NIV).

- **Proverbs 18:6,7**   A *fool's* lips bring him strife, and his mouth invites a beating. A *fool's* mouth is his undoing, and his lips are a snare to his soul (NIV).

- **Ecclesiastes 5:3**   A *fool's* voice is known by his many words.

The apostle James claimed that the tongue is an untameable, unruly evil, full of poison and set on fire by hell. Stubborn fools verify that those words are true. These fools hide their hatred with hypocritical lies and utter slander in the next breath. Their mouths feed on contention, rebellion and strife, so much so that their words invite beatings.

- **Proverbs 9:13**   The woman *Folly* is loud; she is undisciplined and without knowledge (NIV).

- **Proverbs 17:24**   A discerning man keeps wisdom in view, but a *fool's* eyes wander to the ends of the earth (NIV).

- **Proverbs 23:9**   Do not speak in the hearing of a *fool*, for he will despise the wisdom of your words.

- **Proverbs 28:26**   He who trusts in himself is a *fool*, but he who walks in wisdom is kept safe (NIV).

- **Psalm 92:5,6**   How great are your works, O LORD, how profound your thoughts! The senseless man does not know, *fools* do not understand (NIV).

Stubborn fools are not interested in the eternal perspective. They recklessly lean on their own minds and hearts, despising godly instruction. Operating ac-

cording to a temporal value system, they believe that
because sin is popular it must be okay. They often can
be heard to say, "Hey, everybody's doing it!"

- **Proverbs 29:11**   A *fool* gives full vent to his anger, but a
                        wise man keeps himself under control
                        (NIV).

- **Proverbs 17:12**   Better to meet a bear robbed of her cubs
                        than a *fool* in his *folly* (NIV).

- **Proverbs 14:33**   What is in the heart of *fools* is made
                        known.

Stubborn fools have uncontrollable tempers. Rage
resides in their inward parts. Every time something
doesn't go their way, they become wild-eyed with fury.

- **Proverbs 13:16**   A *fool* exposes his *folly* (NIV).

Stubborn fools enjoy their folly and flaunt it, even
though it is disgusting to others.

Fools cannot defer gratification. They are driven
by lust and its attendant vices, impatience and selfish-
ness. You name it, they want it. Sex. Money. Status.
Their motto is, "I want it and I want it now! And I don't
care who I hurt in the process."

Denial of selfish lusts is a key to successful living.
Stubborn fools, however, refuse to "just say no" to any
of their self-centered desires. Like emotionally immature thirteen-year-olds, they want the benefits of
adulthood without its responsibilities. Aware that
something is lacking in their character, they continually
try to fill the emptiness inside. It's sad, though, because
they hate the instruction that would give them ultimate
fulfillment.

- **Proverbs 13:19**   *Fools* detest turning from evil (NIV).

- **Proverbs 26:11**   As a dog returns to his own vomit, so a *fool* repeats his *folly* (NIV).

- **Proverbs 1:32**   The complacency of *fools* will destroy them.

- **Proverbs 13:20**   He who walks with the wise grows wise, but a companion of *fools* suffers harm.

The benefit of a friendship can be evaluated with a question: Who is affecting whom? The careless ease and complacency of stubborn fools affect simple and unreasonable fools so much that it can morally destroy them. Granted, we cannot live in insulated bubbles, free from the world's contamination. But we must be careful, because befriending one who has entered into stubborn foolishness can be dangerous to our own moral sanity.

How Stubborn Foolishness Is Treated

- **Proverbs 17:10**   A rebuke impresses a man of discernment more than a hundred lashes a *fool*.

- **Proverbs 19:29**   Judgments are prepared for scoffers, and beatings for the backs of *fools*.

- **Proverbs 26:3**   A whip for a horse, a halter for the donkey, and a rod for the backs of *fools*!

Even though for the most part stubborn fools will not accept rebuke, approval of their stubbornness must not be tolerated. Major reproof is necessary. Paul told Timothy that when he rebuked anyone, he must do it with long-suffering and doctrine. Simply put, the reproof must be characterized by patience and a stubborn fool must be given clear guidance so he doesn't continue in his ungodly direction.

- **Proverbs 14:7**   Go from the presence of a *foolish* man,

when you do not perceive in him the
lips of knowledge.

After explaining the precise points of error, wise
people leave the presence of stubborn fools who possess lips and hearts that are void of knowledge.

- **Proverbs 3:35**   The wise inherit honor, but *fools* he
                      [God] holds up to shame.

- **Proverbs 26:1**   Like snow in summer or rain in har-
                      vest, honor is not fitting for a *fool*.

- **Proverbs 26:8**   Like tying a stone in a sling is the
                      giving of honor to a *fool*.

Shame is the highest rank for stubborn fools.
Honor should never be conferred upon them. In other
words, they make terrible deacons or elders in a church.

- **Ecclesiastes 10:12** A *fool* is consumed by his own lips
                      (NIV).

Self-inflicted wounds ultimately swallow them up.
They heap problems on themselves and then wonder
why things are going wrong.

Summary

This is a much more serious category of foolishness than the simple or unreasonable fool. The stubborn
fool has allowed his selfish appetites to remain un-
checked. He cares little about God's estimation
regarding his lifestyle and unashamedly pursues the
pleasures of this world. This fool's boldness with
regards to sin is frightening.

Points to Ponder

1. In 1 Samuel 26:21, King Saul admits to David that

he is a stubborn fool. What evidence from Saul's life would support his confession?

2. Do you see any characteristics of the stubborn fool in your life? What can you do to help eliminate them?

Laughing Hyenas

*You have laughed God out of your schools,
out of your books, and out of your life,
but you cannot laugh Him out of your death.
—Dagobert Runes*

Laughing hyenas. Found throughout Africa, these spotted, dog-like scavengers are capable of astonishing boldness. They are especially daring when food is scarce. Above all, they are probably best known for their giggle. I am told that it consists of a series of high-pitched "hee-hee-hee's" that resemble wild laughter.

Hyenas remind me of mocking fools. *Lûwts,*[1] the Hebrew term for this type of fool, literally means "to make mouths at"—in other words, to scorn or to have in derision. These individuals are irreverent, impudent people who scoff at the most sacred precepts set forth in Scripture.

They are also hyena-like in the brazen manner with which they attempt to destroy the holy. They will throw barbed insults, flippant remarks or silent contempt at anyone who wants to live for God. It is hard to understand, but sometimes church folk engage in hyena-like behavior.

How to Detect Mocking Foolishness

* **Proverbs 13:1**   A wise son heeds his father's instruction, but a *mocker* does not listen to rebuke (NIV).

Mocking fools do not handle rebuke well. In fact, they are so sure of themselves that they refuse to listen to reproof, even from their own fathers.

* **Proverbs 14:6**   The *mocker* seeks wisdom and finds none, but knowledge comes easily to the discerning (NIV).

They seek for wisdom in vain because their cavalier attitudes blind them and deafen them to spiritual matters.

* **Proverbs 21:24**   The proud and arrogant man—"*Mocker*" is his name; he behaves with overweening pride (NIV).

Mocking fools carry an elitist, exclusive mindset that ultimately disdains anyone who doesn't advance their private ambitions.

* **Proverbs 1:22**   How long will *mockers* delight in *mockery*? (NIV)

* **Proverbs 24:9**   Men detest a *mocker* (NIV).

Mocking fools are obnoxious and an abomination to others. Intelligent people ultimately tire of their jeering comments. The response that begins with a conspiratorial smirk soon becomes, "Hey, I'm tired of your sarcastic attitude. What's your problem?"

- **Proverbs 15:12**   A *mocker* resents correction; he will not consult the wise (NIV).

Mocking fools hate those who dare to rebuke them. It is an affront to their presumptuous vanity. If you disagree with their philosophy of life, they will respond with exaggerated indignation. Because of pride, they refuse to go to wise people for any type of counsel.

- **Psalm 1:1**   Blessed is the man who does not walk in the counsel of the wicked or stand in the way of sinners or sit in the seat of *mockers* (NIV).

The old adage, "Birds of a feather flock together," is true about mocking fools. They are surrounded by like-minded people. They are best known by the company they keep.

How Mocking Foolishness Is Treated

- **Proverbs 19:25**   Flog a *mocker,* and the simple will learn prudence (NIV).
- **Proverbs 21:11**   When a *mocker* is punished, the simple gain wisdom (NIV).
- **Proverbs 22:10**   Drive out the *mocker,* and out goes strife; quarrels and insults are ended (NIV).

Mocking fools are to be treated with tough love. Just mention "church discipline," though, and some individuals throw their hands up in horror. We've already touched on the necessity of church discipline, so I'd just like to add a few more thoughts.

The place of church discipline is seldom questioned by those who understand and are willing to obey the Scriptures in this matter. Church discipline was never designed by God to function as a political mechanism for silencing legitimate objection or to handle common disagreements. It becomes necessary only when there are clearly unresolved issues, e.g., *continuing* immorality and disorderliness, *persistent* teaching of false doctrine, *unresolvable* disputes between members. The operative words are *continuing, persistent* and *unresolvable*.

In *The Call for Church Discipline*,[2] Paul Van Gorder reveals three reasons church discipline is absolutely necessary when a mocking fool flaunts his or her right to continue in sin:

1. It is essential for the glory of God and the honor of His name.

2. It not only benefits the individual, but it also serves as a graphic warning to those operating in simple foolishness.

3. It is exercised to keep the church pure.

Sin is contagious. The Bible says that a little leaven leavens the whole lump. Leaven is not simply referring to evil, but *evil allowed*. And as Van Gorder says, if the evil sponsored by a mocker is allowed to remain in an assembly of believers, it will not be long until its damaging and putrefying effects will spread throughout the whole body.

Perhaps we're afraid of church discipline because so few instances have resulted in positive change. I have often wondered why there have been so very few restorations of fallen people in church dealings. Why are fallen leaders hardly ever heard from again? Were they hard-hearted? Did God just let them go?

Harold J. Brokke put his finger on the heart of this issue:

When *man* deals with sin, he seeks to discover the wrong. He tends to make those wrongs public, and then he uses others' blunders and sins for personal advantage. Ultimately, God is not even welcome in one of the battles.

Then Brokke adds:

When *Christ* deals, He is slow to expose. He writes our wrongs in dust rather than in stone. He deals with the accusers by saying that the first one who has a right to cast a stone is the one who is without sin.[3]

It is from the you-who-are-spiritual-should-restore-him-gently perspective that Christ would have us deal with mocking fools. Unfortunately, though, mocking fools are so far from the light that most efforts, no matter how tender or gentle, will fail. That is one of the heartaches that plagues a spirit-filled leader—people who refuse genuine help.

- **Proverbs 9:7,8**   Whoever corrects a *mocker* invites insult; whoever rebukes a wicked man incurs abuse. Do not rebuke a *mocker* or he will hate you; rebuke a wise man and he will love you (NIV).

- **Proverbs 13:1**   A wise son heeds his father's instruction, but a *mocker* does not listen to rebuke (NIV).

Since mocking fools won't listen to rebuke even from their own fathers, they certainly won't tolerate it from anyone else. If someone reprehends them, mocking fools will hate that person so much that they will expend great amounts of energy to shame them in the public eye.

Driven by bizarre, almost demonic energy, nothing will stop mockers until they put an indelible stain

on the character of the one who has reproved them.
Scripture warns against rebuking mockers. Godly wisdom and timing are required when expelling mocking
fools from church fellowship.

- **Psalm 1:1**   Blessed is the man who does not . . . sit
                         in the seat of *mockers* (NIV).

Christians are called to be light and salt in an evil
world, but we are also warned not to fellowship with
these murmuring hearts. Bluntly put, get away and stay
away from them. Simple fools often became sentimen-
tal and try to help mockers by befriending them. But
the simple are not able to cope with this sophisticated
form of evil. The best way to assist a mocking fool is to
obey the clear instruction given in Psalm 1:1.

- **Proverbs 3:34**   [God] mocks proud *mockers* but gives
                         grace to the humble (NIV).

- **Proverbs 19:29**   Penalties are prepared for *mockers* (NIV).

- **Isaiah 29:20**   The ruthless will vanish, the *mockers*
                         will disappear, and all who have an eye
                         for evil will be cut down (NIV).

If there is no repentance, punishment is fixed and
ready by God for mockers. He resists mockers every
step of the way.

Summary

Mockers don't seem to enjoy any type of unity, unless they form a coalition with like-minded people who
delight in destroying godly influences. The casual observer is easily deceived by the intellect and strategy of
mocking fools as they conspire together to overthrow
those in legitimate positions of authority. When causing
division, they are known to employ any form of deceit.

Points to Ponder

1. What is your response to the concept of church discipline? Why? If you have observed an effective use of church discipline, what were its main components?

2. What are the dangers of disciplining a mocking fool? How would you handle such a fool if he were a co-worker or family member?

Lemmings to the Sea

It is not wise to argue with a fool because someone may come by and not be able to tell who is who.
—Bernard Meltzer

I was incredulous. My young, impressionable, fifteen-year-old mind was awed by the chilling scene before my eyes. Thousands of tiny, mouse-like animals were blindly swarming over the edge of a cliff to certain death in the crashing waves below.

The television program I was watching detailed the mystery of the suicidal death marches of the Scandinavian rodents called lemmings. The commentator stated that the name lemming is a Norwegian word which means "destroying," referring to the ravages the animals would leave behind after a mass migration.

The commentator theorized that this suicide phenomenon happened whenever the population reached a peak. The numbers of these furry creatures would become so great that all vegetation in the region would be consumed, meaning the horde faced certain starvation. In vast numbers they would begin to travel in almost any direction, but once on the way they continued in a straight path. They entertained no detours or changes in direction. Though thousands may perish, they walked straight into a fast-flowing river or over the edge of a precipice.

These lemmings remind me of the deliberate blindness of committed fools. Even when confronted by the claims and extra-biblical evidences regarding the reliability of Scripture, these fools march on in lemming-like style toward certain destruction. No amount of warnings or intellectual reasoning can stop them. Don't confuse them with facts. They are committed to evil.

Committed fools have regressed to the point of apostasy. The Hebrew word, *nâbâl*,[1] literally means wicked, impious and vile. Other meanings include: to wilt, fall away, fail, faint, despise, be morally deficient, disgrace, dishonor, lightly esteem and abandon. The picture this word paints is that of an empty bag made of animal skin. It has collapsed because the contents have spilled onto the ground.

How to Detect Committed Foolishness

• **Psalm 53:1**   The *fool* says in his heart, "There is no God." They are corrupt, their ways are vile; there is no one who does good.

Imagine this. Committed fools impudently proclaim, "There is no God." Ever heard some learned people spout off that statement? Chances are, they fall into this category of foolishness. They are the ones who make bold, grandiose statements against God and against those who truly represent Him. Their mouths are filled with words sponsored by evil.

• **Genesis 34:7**   Now Jacob's sons had come in from the

fields as soon as they heard what happened. They were filled with grief and
fury, because Shechem had done a disgraceful thing [*folly*] in Israel by lying
with Jacob's daughter—a thing that
should not be done.

Shechem, the Hivite ruler, raped Jacob's daughter.
The defilement of Dinah was motivated by committed
foolishness. The grief, rage and disgust her brothers felt
reveals the depth of evil Shechem had entered into.

- **Judges 20:5b,6**   They raped my concubine, and she
  died. I took my concubine, cut her into
  pieces and sent one piece to each
  region of Israel's inheritance, because
  they committed this lewd and disgraceful act [*folly*] in Israel.

A Levite and his wife were travelling from Beth-
lehem back to their home located in a remote area of the
hill country of Ephraim. Late one evening they found
themselves in Gibeah, a town just five miles north of
Jerusalem. No rooms were to be found, so they sat
dejectedly in the town square wondering what to do
next. An old man took pity on them and invited them
over to his house to stay. Just after settling in for the
evening, they were startled by the sounds of fists
pounding on the door and the shouts of men from the
tribe of Benjamin.

"Bring out the man who came to your house so we
can have sex with him," the Benjamites cried.

"No," the man replied. "Don't be so vile! Look,
you can have my virgin daughter and the man's wife.
You can use them in any way you wish."

The men wouldn't listen and increased their
threats. So the Levite pushed his concubine out to them.

They savagely raped and abused her throughout the night. Next morning she was found dead.

The Levite cut her brutalized body into twelve pieces and sent those parts to the tribes of Israel from Dan to Beersheba, along with the horrible story of her death. Outraged by this unrestrained act of wickedness, the rest of the tribes of Israel allied their forces against the unrepentant tribe of Benjamin. The Benjamites were virtually wiped out. Twenty-five thousand of their prime swordsmen were killed in one day and all their towns were destroyed by fire.

The men of the tribe of Benjamin can be classified as committed fools.

- **2 Samuel 13:11-13** But when [Tamar] took [bread] to [Amnon] to eat, he grabbed her and said, "Come to bed with me, my sister." "Don't, my brother!" she said to him. "Don't force me. Such a thing should not be done in Israel! Don't do this wicked thing [*folly*]. What about me? Where could I get rid of my disgrace? And what about you? You will be like one of the wicked *fools* in Israel."

Amnon, the son of King David, fell in love with his beautiful sister, Tamar. Amnon desired to have sex with his sister and hatched a plot to fulfill his passions. Pretending to be sick, he asked for Tamar to come and cook for him. With the aroma of freshly baked bread in the air, he ordered everyone else to leave the room and stated his intentions to Tamar. Refusing to listen to her protests, he overpowered and raped her. It is interesting to note that once his lust was satisfied, his hatred toward her was more intense than any affection he had felt prior to this hideous act.

- **Joshua 7:15**   He who is caught with the devoted things shall be destroyed by fire, along with all that belongs to him. He has violated the covenant of the Lord and has done a disgraceful thing [*folly*] in Israel.

Against God's command, Achan hid precious items from the recently demolished Jericho. His behavior was classified in the committed category of foolishness. The Israelites were to place all articles of silver, gold, bronze and iron into the treasury of the Lord's house. Achan was directly disobedient to God and was ultimately stoned to death with his entire family. God also punished Israel with a military setback at Ai.

- **1 Samuel 25:25**   May my lord [King David] pay no attention to the wicked man *Nabal*. He is just like his name—his name is *Fool*, and *folly* goes with him.

Nabal, whose name literally means committed fool, was married to a beautiful woman named Abigail. He had acquired much wealth from raising sheep and goats in Carmel. David and his men were encamped in the Wilderness of Paran. With a bunch of hungry soldiers on his hands, David sent a messenger to Nabal requesting food. Even though David's men had protected all of Nabal's property, including his sheep shearers, Nabal responded to the request with wicked, vile insults.

David got mad! As he gathered his troops to squash Nabal, Abigail intervened, meeting David while he was still on the warpath. She had gracious words along with enough food to fill many stomachs. After David's temper was mollified, she returned home and gave Nabal the good news the next day after he had gotten over his drunken stupor. Ten days later, Nabal became ill and died. God had a direct hand in his death.

• **Job 42:7,8**

> After the Lord has spoken these things to Job, he said to Eliphaz, the Temanite, "I am angry with you and your two friends, because you have not spoken of me what is right, as my servant Job has. So now take seven bulls and seven rams and go to my servant Job and sacrifice a burnt offering for yourselves. My servant Job will pray for you, and I will accept his prayer and not deal with you according to your *folly*."

Surprisingly, Job's three friends were guilty of committed foolishness and they would have been severely punished if Job had not interceded on their behalf. Eliphaz, Bildad and Zophar spoke as supposed representatives of God's thoughts. Job had earlier said, "Will you speak wickedly on God's behalf? Will you speak deceitfully for Him?"

God was angry with these three men and allowed them to condemn themselves. In a certain sense, Bildad was pronouncing his own judgment when he said to Job, "Your enemies will be clothed in shame, and the tents of the wicked shall be no more."

God doesn't take kindly to those who claim to be His special agents and yet speak in a wicked and deceitful manner.

I always had a hard time understanding the severity of God's judgment on Job's three "friends" until I saw the category of folly they were operating under. We know that God looks on the hearts of people. Even though some of their statements were profoundly true, God must have observed something in the motives of Job's friends' hearts that caused Him to deal with them in such a harsh manner.

- **Proverbs 17:21**   To have a *fool* for a son brings grief.

Parents of committed fools have no joy in their children. Their heartache is the result of a sorrow rooted in the human soul. It is the pain of a broken heart.

- **Ezekiel 13:3**   This is what the Sovereign LORD says: "Woe to the *foolish* prophets who follow their own spirit and have seen nothing!"

False religious leaders are subjectively oriented and follow their own wicked hearts. As foolish, blind guides, they subscribe to vain, self-centered philosophies. They reject the inspiration and reliability of the Scriptures.

True leaders, however, base their private faith and public message on the objective, written Word of God. They test ecstatic experiences, dreams and visions by that same Word.

- **Jeremiah 17:11**   Like a partridge that hatches eggs it did not lay is the man who gains riches by unjust means. When his life is half gone, they will desert him, and in the end he will prove to be a *fool*.

Committed fools are opportunists who love taking advantage of people caught in unfortunate circumstances. They are takers, not givers. They manipulate and use so many people that in the end, they are left by themselves. A fool that is wrapped up in himself makes a very small package.

How Committed Foolishness Is Treated

After reading the biblical accounts of Shechem, the Benjamites, Amnon, Achan, Nabal and Job's three pals, it is apparent that God deals harshly with committed fools. Psalm 53, the "fool-hath-said-in-his-heart-there-is-no-God" chapter, accurately describes the heart attitude and activity of this final category of fools.

These fools arrogantly instruct others from their wicked hearts. Don't waste your time with them. Let God deal directly with them. They are not interested in learning about spiritual matters. They are, in fact, committed to teaching you. Their heresy must be categorically rejected. It is wise to have no association with them. They are hell-bent in lemming-like fashion toward destruction.

Their conduct reveals a calculated, planned indifference rather than simple ignorance of God. It is frightening. In Psalm 53, David says that when God appears in judgment, committed fools are overwhelmed with dread. God despises them and puts them to shame.

Let's take a look at the end of some committed fools and beware.

Shechem and his men were tricked into performing the painful rite of circumcision and were then systematically murdered by Dinah's brothers, Simeon and Levi—the masters of cruelty.

The tribe of Benjamin was virtually wiped out by a military coalition comprised of Israel's other tribes.

Two years after Amnon's defilement of Tamar, his brother, Absalom, got him drunk and then engineered Amnon's cold-blooded murder.

Achan and his whole family were stoned to death.

Nabal was struck dead by God just ten days after insulting King David.

Job's three friends were mercifully spared from God's judgment only because of Job's prayer on their behalf.

Committed foolishness is serious business.

Summary

Committed fools have regressed so far in apostasy and rebellion that, for the most part, they no longer feel troubled when warned by the Holy Spirit. It's best to stay away from these fools and let God deal with them. He'll take care of it—as we've seen!

Let's paint a picture now to summarize the development of a fool. I'd like to tell you about a guy I'll call Martin. His speech, behavior and philosophy of life betray his brand of foolishness. There is no doubt about it—he is a committed fool, a wolf of the highest order.

Looking at Martin, you'd never know that he was raised in a religious environment. He boldly proclaims that he is now an atheist. Martin claims to be bound by no moral, theological or philosophical standards. He pretty much does what pleases him. He denies the existence of heaven and hell. In effect, he has become his own god.

If you engage in a theological discussion with him, he will listen rather politely for a while. But then he will rip apart the constructs of your belief system bit by bit. With acerbic wit, disarming smile and extreme intelligence, he attempts to dazzle you with obscure bits of information that have been glued together to buttress his opinions. Any facts you present to counter his views are struck down.

Martin's departure from the light was long and sometimes torturous. No doubt, as a young fellow, he wallowed about as a *simple fool* for quite some time. Living in a Christian environment, complete with Sunday school lessons and daily exposure to Bible stories, he was continually confronted by commandments and principles that seemed to be too much for him. He couldn't attain such a high standard.

He was frustrated with unresolved guilt and had to contend with the never-ending demands of his sensual appetite. Remorse for his sins would strike occasionally, but that was only when he had suffered the negative consequences of getting caught. This persuaded him to enter the concealed realm of sensual fantasies which unmasked a secret envy of those who seemed to "get away with it" all the time.

At about sixteen or seventeen years of age, he entered into *unreasonable foolishness*. He had cultivated a smoldering hatred for several years which now erupted into a volcano of illogical, excessive anger aimed mostly in the direction of his parents but included his family's pastor and some of the more demanding teachers at school as well. During this stage, he periodically compensated for guilt by performing teenage gestures of benevolence.

After leaving home and being on his own, Martin finally felt liberated. No more parental rules and regulations. No more church. No more need for hypocrisy on any level. He was free to live life the way he wanted. He jumped into the realm of *stubborn foolishness* with both feet. But Christian values hounded his conscience, so he expended great energy trying to justify his behavior. Since he was constantly confronted by his upbringing, he had to twist God's principles in order to retain his sanity.

Slowly but surely he became a *mocking fool*. Before he could establish a modern mode of thinking governed by his personal morality, he had to systematically tear down the old. His griping about "moral rigidity" soon degenerated into scoffing. He focused his energy on mocking anything sacred. With a mind corrupted by satanic propaganda, he rejected any efforts to help him and spurned all rebukes.

Now in his late fifties, Martin is a *committed fool*. He is a settled man. He no longer struggles with the tempestuous issues of raging hormones versus moral purity. He is a man at peace with himself. He is not wrestling with youthful notions about a real, personal God and an actual heaven and hell. Those "myths" are for weak people who need a crutch.

There is, in fact, a twinkle in his eye when he laughs—which is often. I am sure that the Holy Spirit has repeatedly offered Martin the option of repentance through the years, but it doesn't appear that he has responded.

How do we deal with the "Martins" in our lives? Wanting to be kind and civil, I choose not to enter into theological debates with people like Martin. Their minds are already made up. While I am not intimidated by their vast amounts of knowledge and experience, I prefer to use my time and energy talking with people who are hungry for the truth.

I've decided to spend my time with the sheep.

Points to Ponder

1. Have you ever talked with someone who claimed that God does not exist? What was your conver-

sation like? What line of reasoning was used to buttress his or her views?

2. Have you ever experienced any aspects of committed foolishness? If so, what caused you to change your direction?

Run Like
a Rat

*People defend nothing more violently than
the pretenses they live by.*
—Allen Drury

Right now you may be feeling a bit overwhelmed.
Those five fools are bad dudes. Facing the hard fact that
there are just plain evil people in the world is not easy.
It may tend to depress you. Or demotivate you. Or,
worse still, cause you to want to just give up.

But I've got some great news: Good is going to tri-
umph over evil. God says so. And He has the plan all
laid out. He wants to teach us how to live among evil
without becoming evil. How to roam among the wolves
and not become one ourselves.

One way he keeps us from evil is by using *guilt*.
Admittedly, many of us carry far more guilt than we
deserve. Satan loves to beat down Christians with false
guilt. But real guilt from the Holy Spirit—that is one of
God's protective devices. It can keep us from repeating
the same mistakes. It can drive us into the arms of our

loving heavenly Father. It can save us from foolishly getting ourselves deeper and deeper into sin.

We'll take a look at guilt and how we are to respond to it in our lives.

A Study in Rat Behavior

I pioneered my very first church in a small fishing village situated on the rugged coast of Maine. We met in what used to be a white-shuttered, little red school-house. One room was heated during the winter by a pot-bellied stove in the corner. Since there wasn't an outhouse, you had to do a lot of planning before coming to church. If someone was desperate, though, a mad dash into the nearby woods was acceptable.

Friday evenings during the summer months were special. The congregation, made up primarily of lobstermen, clam diggers, boat builders, fishermen and their families, filed into the little red schoolhouse. After about twenty minutes of robust singing and worship, we settled down and I taught a lesson from the Bible. When the clock struck nine, however, the lesson was promptly over. I vacated the premises with a very special destination in mind—the town dump.

Some of the guys piled into the car with me and we tooled our way over the winding back roads. Within ten minutes we turned onto the pot-holed lane that led us to the garbage heap. We were about to enjoy our favorite evening pastime—shooting rats at the town dump.

We taped high-powered, four-celled flashlights to the barrels of our .22 rifles so that they hung snugly beneath. Excitedly we loaded the guns, spaced ourselves evenly on one side and pointed our lethal spotlights in the direction of the ghostly mounds of trash.

Immediately, I saw a pair of beady, red eyes reflecting the piercing beam of light aimed in its direction. I shot and missed. The long-tailed rodent was too fast for my reflexes. Scanning the territory assigned to me, I located another set of eyes, aimed and fired. A direct hit.

As the evening progressed, our marksmanship skills were increasingly challenged. Our moving targets were becoming craftier with each passing minute. The roving floodlights made them jumpy. As soon as they saw the light, they scrambled for cover under a smashed stereo or behind a scrunched-up washing machine.

What happened many years ago on those moonlit evenings is a crude reminder of the natural bent of human behavior. Much like rats, we gravitate toward darkness and filth. Even though we have trouble admitting it, we actually love darkness rather than light.

When God's searchlight reveals the true nature of our hearts, we tend to blame someone else, cover up with fig leaves, or run and hide. Fleeing from the Holy Spirit's conviction seems harmless initially, but over a period of time we become first-class hypocrites filled with self-deception. We flee from the very One who can deliver us from the gnawing basic problems in our lives.

Our Options in Dealing With Guilt

As human beings, we have a natural desire to learn about evil. God wants us to have inquisitive minds on most subjects, but with evil it is different. He wants us to know about evil not by experience, but by developing a healthy understanding from the Bible on the subject. If we're taught by the Word of God, anything less than God's truth will stick out like a sore thumb. It will be exposed automatically for what it truly is—evil and a lie.

If, however, we meddle with evil, we are quickly enticed away from eternal values by our lustful, "I-want-it-now" desires. Our attention becomes focused on sensual fulfillment. Just as Eve questioned God's specific commands when Satan tempted her in the Garden of Eden, we begin the foolish act of calling scriptural instructions into question. Old-fashioned principles just don't seem to apply to the sin-soaked challenges of this modern era.

As the carnal, sensual focus persists, our unabated lust becomes pregnant with desire. Our overwhelming desire is conveniently matched by a carefully orchestrated opportunity. Like rats, we run from the light straight into the deceptive shadows.

At some point, our conscience is violated by the act of sin and we are stirred suddenly by wretched pangs of guilt. Since our emotional system wasn't designed to bear this pressure, we respond in one of four ways:

1. We rationalize the guilt away: "Oh, it was just a mistake. I wasn't myself today."

2. We do good deeds to compensate for our sin: "I felt much better after helping at the soup kitchen all afternoon."

3. We chastise ourselves: "Maybe if I am depressed long enough, God will see how sorry I am."

4. We confess our sins to the One who knows everything about us and still loves us: "Jesus, please forgive me for sinning against You."

The fourth option, of course, is the only one that

leaves us with a clear conscience and in right relation-ship with God.

When guilt twinges our conscience, we've come to an absolutely crucial point of decision. We can either run like a rat from the light or we can run boldly to the throne of grace. It ultimately is a choice between foolishness and wisdom.

How we handle real guilt is a factor in determining whether we'll tend toward the light or head for the darkness. Incomplete repentance will push us in the run-like-a-rat direction of some category of foolishness. It will cause us to start down the road to wolfdom, swinedom, snakedom or ratdom. On the other hand, if we acknowledge our guilt and allow it to be confronted by the Word, the Spirit and the blood, we will be safe as sheep in the arms of Jesus Christ, our gentle Shepherd.

Points to Ponder

1. Have you ever spent futile hours trying to illuminate the spirit of someone who is determined to run from the light? Do you think you crossed the line between lighting a candle to show the right path and using your lantern to chase rats in the dark?

2. When the Holy Spirit convicts you of sin, how do you handle the guilt?

Harumph!

It is well, when judging another person, to remember that he is judging you with the same god-like and superior impartiality.
—Arnold Bennett

It's time now to shift our focus. We've already defined the problem (two-legged wolves, serpents and swine exist), so now we're going to look at some positive solutions. Let's point the finger right back at ourselves and begin there. We need to talk about the dangers of a judgmental spirit.

"Harumph!" Can you hear the tone of voice? Gruff. Throaty. Emphatic. Dripping with disdain. How about the face? Squinted eyes. Teeth clenched. Lips pursed together. What about the person? Rigid. Opinionated. Insecure. Nitpicky.

There is a lot going on in this person's restricted internal world. He rarely, if ever, gives himself permission to experience the liberty of God's forgiveness. Life makes demands and he responds from behind the barbed wire of critical suspicion and petty concerns. He survives by reducing life to a certain set of predictable rules and regulations. He serves an austere Master, lives in an inflexible world and carefully cultivates a countenance that screams, "HARUMPH!"

Chuck Swindoll, in his must-read book *The Grace Awakening*, relates a story that describes a person of a different sort:

> During his days as president, Thomas Jefferson and a group of companions were traveling across the country on horseback. They came to a river which had left its banks because of a recent downpour. The swollen river had washed the bridge away. Each rider was forced to ford the river on horseback, fighting for his life against the rapid currents. The very real possibility of death threatened each rider, which caused a traveler who was not a part of their group to step aside and watch.
>
> After several had plunged in and made it to the other side, the stranger asked President Jefferson if he would ferry him across the river. The president agreed without hesitation. The man climbed on, and shortly thereafter the two of them made it safely to the other side.
>
> As the stranger slid off the back of the saddle on to dry ground, one in the group asked him, "Tell me, why did you select the president to ask this favor of?" The man was shocked, admitting he had no idea it was the president who had helped him. "All I know," he said, "is that on some of your faces was written the answer 'No,' and on some of them was the answer 'Yes.' His was a 'Yes' face."[1]

If you were that stranger, what would have attracted you to the president? What would you have watched for before entrusting your life in his hands?

Thomas Jefferson was not even aware that he was under such scrutiny. He must have unknowingly expressed a confidence, strength and poise. Like President Jefferson, there may be times in our lives when we're not aware of the impact we're making on others. Yet we all have a sphere of influence regardless of how high or low a profile we keep.

Without a doubt, Jesus had a "Yes" face. He attracted all types of people. Playful children. Jaded tax collectors. Hopeless prostitutes. Blind beggars. Even some Pharisees with honest questions. At the same time He was surrounded by pompous, religious men whose wells had long ago been poisoned by judgment and legalism. Their every action and attitude cried, "Harumph!"

We have a choice. We can either be like Jesus and draw people to Him or we can settle into a Pharisaical "harumphing" and drive hungry souls away from their provision. Your answers to these pointed questions will help you determine your tendency to "harumph."

- When you do what you do, do you dispense grace?
- Are the people you serve given the freedom to be who they are, or who you expect them to be?
- Do you let others go or do you smother and control them?
- Do folks feel intimidated or relieved in your presence?
- Are you cultivating spontaneous, creative celebrants or fearful captives?
- Do you encourage, build up and affirm those to whom you minister?
- Are you one who models grace or not?
- Is what you're doing the work of your own flesh energized by your own strength?
- Do you often have a hidden agenda?
- Is the enhancement of your image of major importance to you?
- Can you honestly say that your work is directed and empowered by the Spirit of God?
- Is yours a "grace awakening" ministry?[2]

Whew! A bunch of those questions hit me where it hurts. I don't know about you, but I struggle at times with a critical spirit. My wife will tell you that when I get perturbed about someone or something, she'll say, "Let the 'harumphing' begin." One particular occasion comes to mind.

My Pal Charlie

The church I was pastoring consisted of a congregation that was just right—not too big and not too small. I was working closely with a guy I'll call Charlie. He was a "pistol." He was a very hard man to reason with. At that phase of my life, I didn't have the emotional maturity to confront his strong personality.

He was able to run roughshod over me at will. I would "wimp out" on cue and then bottle my feelings. Afterward, I would go home and dump my foul attitude on my wife. At the time, I didn't realize the full ramifications of my judgmental spirit, nor could I discern how my "harumphing" was infecting my wife's morale.

We "ate" well during those months. Just about every day we dined on "broiled Charlie" for breakfast, "fried Charlie" for lunch and "roasted Charlie" for dinner. For dessert we often had "frozen Charlie" or "lemon Charlie pie."

I was just sure that Charlie knew there was tension between us, but for the most part he seemed oblivious to the fact that I was troubled. I masterfully masked my increasing contempt for him and his opinions.

Then I made a mistake. I began teaching a verse-by-verse series on the book of James during our midweek meetings. The conviction from the Holy Spirit reached a rolling boil by the time I hit the second chapter of James. I got nailed between the eyes by James 2:13: "For judgment is without mercy to the one who has shown no mercy. Mercy triumphs over judgment."

I can clearly remember the discomfort I experienced during the hours spent studying this passage in preparation for the evening meeting. I am prone to taking theological "rabbit trails" when studying a particular verse, and I took one of those trails that day. For the first time I began to understand that while God hates a lot of things, He tends to harbor a special hatred for judgmental attitudes that seem to automatically trigger the sins of the tongue. Hang in there with me while we investigate some of the verses I discovered that pinpoint this issue. I've also added some of the thoughts I had about my pal Charlie as I read and studied each verse.

For none of us lives to himself alone and none of us dies to himself alone. If we live, we live to the Lord; and if we die, we die to the Lord. So, whether we live or die, we belong to the Lord. For this very reason, Christ died and returned to life so that he might be the Lord of both the dead and the living. You, then, why do you judge your brother? Or why do you look down on your brother? For we will all stand before God's judgment seat (Romans 14:7-10, NIV).

Charlie and I have the responsibility of working together in at least a civil fashion. Everyone, including me, has strengths and weaknesses. Charlie is not accountable ultimately to me. I'm blaming him for my reactions. Actually, I'm the one with the problem. God probably ordained this situation from before the foundation of the world. Charlie's personality is being used to smoke out some stuff in my heart that I'll have to confront down the road anyway. I might as well deal with it now. My main responsibility is not for Charlie's actions, but for my attitude toward him. I will have to answer to God some day, and my bad-attitude excuses won't cut it. He'll look me straight in the eye and say, "Oh stop it, Joel." Nope, I won't be able to sneak anything by Him.

You, therefore, have no excuse, you who pass judgment on someone else, for at whatever point you judge the other, you are condemning yourself, because you who pass judgment do the same things (Romans 2:1, NIV).

This verse makes me mad. The more I think about it, why can't I have an excuse? Why is the spotlight on me? Look at Charlie. He's like a steamroller, squashing anyone who gets in his path and disagrees with him. How can his personality honor God? Someone has to set him straight. Maybe it was ordained that I was to be put in his path to stop him in his tracks.

Wait a minute. I need to look at this more closely. The focus is still on my heart. Look at the way Paul says that I am guilty of doing the same things. The list of sins in Romans 1 is a mixed bag. Murder, homosexuality and adultery are put in the same category as being unmerciful, harboring unforgiveness, lacking discernment and ripping someone up behind his back. Whew! This puts a whole new spin on things. According to this, I cannot categorize sins, jump into my ivory tower and then "harumph" behind closed doors about the Charlies in my life. In God's economy, I am guilty of doing the same things and worse.

Do not judge, or you too will be judged. For in the same way you judge others, you will be judged, and with the measure you use, it will be measured to you. Why do you look at the speck of sawdust in your brother's eye and pay no attention to the plank in your own eye? You hypocrite, first take the plank out of your own eye, and then you will see clearly to remove the speck from your brother's eye (Matthew 7:1-3,5, NIV).

This is the only way I know that a person can be disciplined for a sin that he may not even be interested in commiting! The moment I judge Charlie, I step out of fellowship with God and am under divine self-induced discipline. I see here a case for a double-barreled blast of discipline. When I say, "Charlie is a proud ego-maniac," it's probably a true statement, but whatever God uses to discipline a proud ego-maniac jumps off Charlie and onto me. My sin will be judged with the same severity I judged Charlie. If I judge Charlie for, let's say, a fifty-gallon sin, fifty gallons of discipline for that sin will flow in my direction. I determine how great my misery will be. I'm stopping this right now. I don't want to bring more trouble my way. Lord, forgive me.

It was at this juncture that I permitted the Holy Spirit to penetrate my heart. What a wonderful memory! I first went to Laurie and asked for her forgiveness. We both knelt down and did business with God. We then set up a plan.

I have given my wife permission to confront me if and when I start "harumphing" about someone or something. And Laurie has granted me permission to stop the direction and tone of her words if I sense a judgmental, critical attitude toward someone she is coping with.

Getting Things Right With Charlie

So what did I do with Charlie? Dealing with people like Charlie is a common occurrence, and usually the problem in a situation like this one is a personality clash. Categorize my problem with Charlie as Joel Freeman's neurotic reactions to a blustery temperament style.

I was hesitant to openly confess my feelings to Charlie with a line like, "You don't know this, but I have hated you for quite a while now." In confrontive situations like that, the other party is usually shocked to say the least. And even though the trouble may be cleared up on a verbal level, it is rare for things to ever be the same as before. I think there is a better way to bring closure in situations like this.

With Charlie, I decided to keep my mouth shut. I didn't bare my soul to him regarding my previous foul attitude. Instead, my new-found resolve to stop judging him was to be implemented. I was going to be obedient to the clear directives I had discovered in God's Word. Prayer became my secret passion. But I wasn't praying for Charlie to change. I prayed for his health, his family, his safety and his career goals.

I cannot explain *how* it happened. I can merely report *what* happened. My heart began to change toward Charlie. Oh, sure, there were still some things about him that irked me. He was rather rough around the edges, and he still possessed the tendency to classify people and situations as either all gold or all dirt. In spite of all that, I experienced a growing appreciation and love for him.

Our working relationship took a turn for the better. Several months later, we were talking over lunch. What started out as "Let's grab a quick bite" soon became "Oops, where has the time gone?" He opened up and shared some deep hurts encountered during his younger years.

I was amazed by the ease of our conversation. It *flowed*. I was thrilled with the level of intimacy we had touched. No question about it, God was performing a miracle before our very eyes. May the devil "harumph!"

Charlie is now living in another city, working in another church. We still keep in touch and have enjoyed a friendship that has survived both time and distance.

What Charlie Taught Me

Charlie was good for me. I learned some valuable lessons from our friendship that have helped me retain a "yes" face in my relationships with others:

1. The things that bug me about another person are usually the same negative characteristics I have not confronted in my own life.

2. I am in constant, dire need of God's mercy, patience and grace.

3. I cannot judge another person and truly pray for him or her at the same time.

4. If I foster a bitter spirit when a man has done or said something that has troubled me and if I talk negatively about him behind his back—even if I'm right about the facts—I'm wrong. My attitude stinks. When I'm tempted to gossip, I try breathing through my nose.

5. True spirituality does not lie in my ability to expose another's faults. Rather, it lies in my passion for the restoration of that person's fellowship with Jesus.

6. I admire and respect God's justice from afar, but wallow in His mercy up close and personal.

7. When someone I respect blows it in my presence

by expressing inappropriate rage or by letting loose with a few four-letter words, I am faced with a spiritual challenge. Either I mentally judge this person because my image of him has been crushed, or I say a quick prayer, "Lord, I am amazed that You think I am spiritually mature enough to handle this situation. Help me to look beyond his faults and see his needs. Give me wisdom and understanding to love him in the same way You love him."

8. The more I grow in Jesus, the more I realize how little I know. I used to have just enough knowledge to be dangerous. Now I realize my understanding is limited. I give advice sparingly.

9. I have a profound respect for every individual's right to make decisions and live with the consequences of those decisions.

10. Someone may get into a problem through a series of bad decisions and may correct the situation through a series of right, biblically-based decisions.

11. My emotions pay the price for my distorted thinking. I experience insecurity, fear and guilt when I fail to confront unrealistic expectations in my relationships with others, such as:

    a. Everyone should understand me.

    b. Everyone should appreciate me and what I do.

    c. Everyone should agree with me.

12. Like me, people tend to be unreasonable, illogical and self-centered. By God's grace, I choose to love anyway.

13. Emotional pain does not inspire maturity. In-

stead, it produces insanity, causing some to say, do and decide things that may go directly against their previously held theological convictions. During these times I am privileged to act or speak in a manner that draws them to Christ. He is the only One who can ultimately touch them in the midst of suffering.

14. I prefer dealing privately with people who have sinned. I get great delight in seeing the ministry of reconciliation taking place when sin is confronted one-on-one. No one else needs to know. I think God smiles when sin is handled in this redemptive fashion.

15. Living a Christ-like life is not hard—it is impossible. I fall at His feet in sublime exhaustion. Instead of living *for* Christ, I permit Him to live *through* me, love *through* me and forgive *through* me.

These home-spun principles are important to me. Our vertical relationship with Jesus is manifested by our horizontal interactions with those around us. When we attempt to ascend to His presence, Jesus keeps pushing us back to earth with words like: "They'll know you are Christians by the way you love one another"; or "A new commandment I give to you, that you love one another as I have loved you."

When You Get the Urge to Harumph

Certain personality types drive us crazy and automatically cause certain prejudices and reactions to gurgle to the surface. At those moments, we may feel an uncontrollable urge to "harumph."

In Proverbs 6:16-19, King Solomon said:

There are six things which the LORD hates, seven which are an abomination to him: haughty eyes, a lying tongue, and hands that shed innocent blood, a heart that devises wicked plans, feet that make haste to run to evil, a false witness who breathes out lies, and a man who sows discord among brothers.

There are some surprises here. A lot of overt sins could have been mentioned in this list. Out of the seven things, though, four of them relate directly to "harumphing":

Haughty eyes

A lying tongue

A false witness who breathes out lies

A man who sows discord among brothers

I really do not think that we can begin to grasp how much God hates a judgmental spirit. I shudder when I think of our tendency to take God's place as judge and our audacity to complain and gripe about everybody and everything that crosses our paths. How arrogant!

Okay, we understand now that we're not to judge. So how do we evaluate the attitudes and actions of others? Hang in there. The next chapter is dedicated to bringing a measure of sanity to this whole mess.

Points to Ponder

1. Who are the people you enjoy "harumphing" about the most? What flaws does this expose in your half of the relationship? How could you support the person who irks you in more positive ways?

2. Review the twelve questions asked near the beginning of this chapter. Do those questions make you turn inward with despair or upward with a sense of hope? Why?

Suspicious Minds

*Most of our suspicions of others are aroused
by our knowledge of ourselves.
—Illinois Journal of Education*

The long distance call came from Kent. "Hey, how are you doing?" he asked. "You popped into my mind and I didn't want the day to sneak by without putting words to my thoughts."

What a pleasant surprise! I leaned back in my chair, shut my eyes and smiled. Kent and I had known each other for several years. We traded small talk about our families, our travels and other interests. And then he embarked on an all-too-familiar story.

For nine months, Kent had been undergoing a horrible experience in his church. Initially, the problem started with a group of women who got together regularly and began discussing the weaknesses of the church. They concluded that the Holy Spirit was grieved with the purpose and direction of that body of believers.

This particular bunch of ladies would arrive on Sunday mornings and cluster together in a section of the sanctuary. While several hundred people were singing and worshipping the Lord, this group would sit in the seats with pained expressions on their faces. It was almost comical. They were "grieving" with the Holy Spirit. During the message, their eyes were tightly closed while their lips were moving as they silently prayed for the pastor's understanding to be enlightened. Their actions were a continual source of heartache to the leadership not to mention the confusion they caused in the congregation. Any attempts to bring about reconciliation were viewed with disdain. It was a no-win situation.

And then the plot thickened. A certain man with a strong personality had been exposed to some controversial teachings about subjects like divorce, remarriage, birth control and Christian contemporary music. It didn't take long for him to hook up with the group of women and fill their pipelines with more negativity. He confronted Kent with his convictions and used the Bible to back up every point. Kent tried to reason with the man, explaining the potential split that could develop in the congregation as a result of these secondary issues, but it did little good.

By now the group of disgruntled members had enlarged and they were increasingly militant. They began to spread nasty rumors about those in leadership, especially Kent. First-time visitors were cornered before leaving the building. Church members were systematically contacted in one way or another. Slowly but surely, the poison spread throughout much of the body.

Kent attempted to counteract all of this with prayer, fasting and magnifying Christ in his preaching. He had already been blunt with the instigators and had shared with the congregation the proper way to handle gossip. Finally, after much emotional pain and agony, he decided to resign as pastor of the church.

At the end of the service the following Sunday, he stood up before the congregation and announced his resignation. The elders were then publicly commissioned by Kent to investigate all charges. His resignation was in force pending the results of their determination. The congregation was shocked.

Five days of intensive research elapsed. The elders uncovered a hornet's nest of bitterness and hidden agendas. It could almost be called a conspiracy. The most unlikely people had become best pals, united by one passion—to destroy those in legitimate spiritual authority. Juvenile attitudes and fleshly tactics were cloaked under the seemingly sincere desire to help keep the church afloat. Hypocrisy and pride abounded. These people seemed to be energized by another force. Their speech, actions and attitudes betrayed the source of their energy—the pit of hell.

Needless to say, the elders gave Kent their endorsement. A number of families left and the church began to experience fresh growth. I rejoiced with Kent as he expressed his renewed commitment to Christ and the church body to which he and his family had been called. He was experiencing a new level of spiritual and emotional maturity. I celebrated with him regarding the new perspective he was given.

The State of the Union

Almost everyone in leadership will confront challenges similar to Kent's. In 1 Corinthians 11:18,19, the apostle Paul declares that at times God permits divisions and factions to be present in a local church. The whole purpose behind this, it seems, is to ensure that those who are genuinely filled with the Holy Spirit and are committed to honoring the Word of God will be plainly recognized by all.

There will always be people who will grumble about the unfairness of church policies. Eventually they may influence a bunch of others to gripe and growl with them. Like a wise old sage once said, "Opinions are like armpits. Everybody's got two of them and they stink most of the time."

But we can't let those negative situations overshadow the fact that people need an environment where they can express ideas, criticisms and complaints without fear of reprisal from those in leadership. We can't expect people to be robots. If two agree on everything, one of them is doing all the thinking. The challenge is to channel those complaints in a biblical, Christ-honoring direction.

Are you regularly a part of a church or Bible study group? If so, have you ever noticed the variety of expectations and viewpoints? People come with special needs and varying emotional pain thresholds. Some have come from backgrounds filled with sexual or physical abuse. A number may have experienced disillusionment at a former church—mismanagement of church funds, pastoral immorality, ultra-authoritarian leadership.

Undoubtedly, these folks will have suspicious minds in any new setting. They will be cynical watchers and skeptics. But if they are surrounded by a loving, non-judgmental environment and sound biblical teaching, they can recover and become vital, productive members of the congregation. Combine teachable spirits with the patient and loving investment of those mature enough to look beyond personal faults, and you'll begin to meet real needs.

I know something about you. There is an invisible sign on your back emblazoned with the words: "Please Don't Judge Me." Everyone is crying out to be loved and accepted for who they are.

I may be idealistic, but I have often thought that Christians ought to be the kindest, most caring community of people in the world. In my opinion, church meetings have the potential of being the most fun-loving, stress-free, yet serious-about-our-purpose-for-being-here gatherings in the universe. Christ has given us the command not to judge. We are not to be wolves intent on picking others apart.

Yet even in my own life I feel prejudices and a judgmental attitude gurgle to the surface of my conscious mind when confronted with certain personality-types or circumstances. It is an automatic knee-jerk, gut-level reaction over which I have little control in its initial stage. I shouldn't be shocked anymore, but sometimes I still am.

"Good" Judgment Versus "Bad" Judgment

Scripture teaches that we can be a part of the solution instead of part of the problem. Let's look at the concept of "judging" in the Bible and determine its place in our lives.

Have you ever noticed while reading the Bible that in some places we are told not to judge and in other sections we are commanded to judge? The original Greek language of the New Testament helps us to sort out the confusion. There are, in fact, two main types of judgment:

1. JUDGMENT—*KRINO*[1] (Bad type): Condemn, conclude, decide, pronounce judgment, punish.

2. DISCERNMENT—*DOKIMAZO, ANAKRINO, DIAKRINO*[2] (Good type): Examine, test, investigate, prove, search out, weigh, distinguish.

We will use the terms *suspicion* or *judgment* for *krino*. The good kind of judgment we will call *discernment*.

We must have all knowledge, be everywhere present and have all power in order to be qualified to sit in judgment of others. Oops, I forgot, we must be perfect as well! Those attributes cancel me and every human being out with regard to the *krino* brand of judgment.

In contrast, we must *all* exercise discernment. Laurie and I have two boys. When they were smaller, we were extremely careful about the reliability, maturity and competence of the babysitters we hired to watch over them. That's a pragmatic level of discernment.

On the spiritual level, I do not blindly accept any teaching that comes down the pike. Like the Bereans in Acts 17:11, we are to "search the scriptures daily, whether those things are so." I am sure that you can think of many other issues that require some form of judgment on our part.

Recently I came across a power-packed booklet, *May Christians Judge?*[3] In it, Mark Pearson does a masterful job of clarifying the difference between discernment and judgment. I have sought his permission and will be borrowing freely from his insights. Let's look at six distinctions between judging (bad type) and discerning (good type). You may find this helpful in testing your own attitudes or actions toward others.

1. JUDGMENT *condemns* others for their visible

problems and fails to realize that those exterior issues stem from inner root problems. The things we hate the most about others are usually the very things we are struggling with ourselves.

Thou that judgest (*krino*) doeth the same things (Romans 2:1).

Why dost thou judge (*krino*) thy brother? (Romans 14:10)

DISCERNMENT *examines self* before presuming to evaluate the actions of others. Only when we have our own spiritual house in order can we act out of humility, as one fellow sinner speaking to another sinner saved by grace.

But let every man prove (*dokimazo*) his own work (Galatians 6:4).

But let a man examine (*dokimazo*) himself (1 Corinthians 11:28).

For if we would judge (*diakrino*) ourselves, we should not be judged (*krino*) (1 Corinthians 11:31).

Prove (*dokimazo*) your own selves (2 Corinthians 13:5).

2. JUDGMENT *forms opinions* on first impressions or hearsay, then looks for evidence to confirm those opinions even though the evidence may be out of context. It is quick to believe something because of its surface appearance.

Judge (*krino*) not according to the appearance (John 7:24).

. . . and judgeth (*krino*) his brother (James 4:11).

Let us not therefore judge (*krino*) one another any more (Romans 14:13).

DISCERNMENT *refrains from forming an opinion* until it has personally verified a story and sought clarification from the parties involved. Second- or third-hand information is selective, emotionally charged and garbled.

Prove (*dokimazo*) all things (1 Thessalonians 5:21).

Try (*dokimazo*) the spirits (1 John 4:1).

He that is spiritual judgeth (*anakrino*) all things (1 Corinthians 2:15).

3. JUDGMENT *deals with matters publicly*. It gossips and maligns and actively seeks to make others judge the person as well. Even if we are able to withstand the obvious temptation to get others on our side, we must still guard against the more subtle temptation to phrase our gossip as a prayer request.

    Judge (*krino*) not and ye shall not be judged (*krino*) (Luke 6:37).

    Speak not evil one of another, brethren (James 4:11).

    DISCERNMENT *deals with the matter privately*. It goes to the person directly and involves no one else.

    Go and tell him his fault between thee and him alone (Matthew 18:15).

    Go thy way; first be reconciled to thy brother (Matthew 5:24).

    Tell it not in Gath, publish it not in the streets of Askelon (2 Samuel 1:20).

4. JUDGMENT *condemns the person* involved. If we cannot approach the person in the same way Jesus handled the woman caught in adultery (see John 8:3-11), it is better to wait until we can. Otherwise, it just might be that our sin in judging will be greater than the sin we are pointing out in the other person.

Wherein thou judgest (*krino*) another, thou condemnest thyself (Romans 2:1).

Who art thou that judgest (*krino*) another? (James 4:12)

DISCERNMENT *condemns the action* but truly loves the person and prays for him or her. It looks beyond the fault and sees the need.

Neither do I condemn thee: go, and sin no more (John 8:11).

Thy sins are forgiven (Luke 7:48).

5. JUDGMENT is *nosey*. It butts in where it has no business being. It is a busybody.

... but tattlers also and busybodies, speaking things which they ought not (1 Timothy 5:13).

... or as a busybody in other men's matters (1 Peter 4:15).

Judge (*krino*) nothing before the time, until the Lord comes (1 Corinthians 4:5).

DISCERNMENT is *respectful of others*, correcting only when necessary. It earns the right to be heard, partly because it doesn't always feel driven to confront. Much of that which is discerned merely fuels quiet but fervent prayer.

Prove (*dokimazo*) all things; hold fast that which is good (1 Thessalonians 5:21).

Let this mind be in you, which was also in Christ Jesus (Philippians 2:5).

6. JUDGMENT *seeks destruction.* When we tear down, we tend to point fingers, glare, use emotive words and speak with a raised voice.

For he shall have judgment (*krisis*) without mercy, that hath showed no mercy (James 2:13).

Their heart studieth destruction (Proverbs 24:2).

The mouth of the foolish is near destruction (Proverbs 10:14).

An hypocrite with his mouth destroyeth his neighbor (Proverbs 11:9).

DISCERNMENT *seeks restoration*. When we build up we tend to speak softly, often with tears and compassion.

Ye which are spiritual, restore such an one in the spirit of meekness (Galatians 6:1).

Let every man be swift to hear, slow to speak, slow to wrath (James 1:19).

A word fitly spoken is like apples of gold in pictures of silver (Proverbs 25:11).

Judge With Pure Motives

Occasionally we, especially those in leadership positions, are required to deliver a strong, sharp prophetic message to someone who has consistently deflected gracious approaches.

The apostle Paul told Titus to be wary of the folks who dwelled in Crete. Titus had been appointed leader over a group of people whom Paul referred to as "liars, evil beasts and lazy gluttons" (Titus 1:12). That's strong language, probably spoken in a dogmatic tone of voice. Titus was told to rebuke them sharply.

The difference between judgment and discernment is not always harsh words versus gentle words. The focus is on motives. Titus wasn't out to tear down those under his leadership or to somehow injure the Cretes in a premeditated fashion. The purpose behind the rebuke was to draw those people to positive repentance so "that they may be sound in the faith" (Titus 1:13).

Think carefully before going to another person to point out his or her faults. Allow the Holy Spirit to search your heart with the light of truth. Ask yourself some questions: Whose needs are getting met? Am I doing this merely because I want to dump on him or her? Is this to tear down or to build up? Be honest.

The Forgotten Aspect of Judging

There's something else to think about. God gave each of us one mouth and two ears. This whole judgment/discernment issue deals with listening as well as speaking.

We all must cope with negativity coming from others. While some innocently express a critical remark about another, many others consistently tear down people and are artists at working a conversation around to the point where they can focus on someone else's blemishes: "I don't know what I'm going to do with Susan"; or "You're the only person I can tell this to"; or "How do you cope with someone you can't stand to be around?" or "I'm concerned about James. We need to pray for him."

If you are a counselor or serve in some other problem-solving position, you have the responsibility to gently challenge wounded individuals to meet privately with the ones who have hurt them. It is important that we protect our hearts by monitoring what we listen to. "Take heed what you hear" is a sobering message straight from the lips of Jesus (see Mark 4:24 and Luke 8:18).

I know how difficult this is to implement. I recognize, however, that it is my responsibility to screen what I allow into my ears. The Institute in Basic Life Principles has provided some helpful information in their paper, *How to Guard Against the Defilement of Listening to an Evil Report* (see Appendix B). One section of the article gives five questions to ask before listening to a potential carrier of an evil report:

1. What is your reason for telling me?

   Widening the circle of gossip only compounds the problem.

2. Where did you get your information?

   Refusal to identify the source of the information is a sure signal of an evil report.

3. Have you gone to those directly involved?

   Spirituality is not measured by how well we expose an offender (see Galatians 6:1).

4. Have you personally checked out all of the facts?

   Even facts become distorted when not balanced with other facts or when given with negative motives.

5. Can I quote you if I check this out?

   Those who give evil reports often claim that they are "misquoted." This is because their words and overriding impressions are reported.[4]

   I have asked people these questions on numerous occasions. When doing so, I carefully avoid using an Houdini-the-Magician gaze and stern tone of voice. I try to be gentle when broaching the subject. Most people are not even aware of the incredibly negative effects of gossip and how much God hates it.

   Sometimes humor can get you out of hearing gossip: "Can you help me? I have a problem with this sort of stuff. Quite frankly, I love gossip. I love to hear every nasty, juicy bit of scandalous rumor. In fact, while waiting in line at the grocery store checkout counter, I constantly fight the urge to pick up one of those sleazy magazines and read about hairy alien women attracting the most eligible earth-bound bachelors."

A wee bit of humor may be the soil that permits a kernel of truth to grow and have sustained impact in the gossiper's life. Sometimes I can lead the humor into a suggestion that the gossiper obey the biblical mandate and go to the offending individual alone. "After all," I ask, "this is how you would want me to treat you if I had a problem with you, isn't it?"

There comes a time when in sublime exhaustion, we resign as masters of the universe. None of us can hide from God's all-knowing, all-caring gaze. Our status as created beings with limited intellect, presence and power disqualifies us from sitting on the judgment seat over others.

The more we fall in love with Jesus, the more we adopt His way of thinking. Jesus possessed the ability to know everything about everyone He met. No one could hate sin more perfectly than He did. Yet we see such a sweet reasonableness about Him. He was always taking risks, always looking to give others the advantage. To the casual observer, He functioned in apparent naiveté at times. Imagine giving Judas Iscariot control of the treasury!

But Jesus was more interested in returning the one lost sheep than He was in exposing its wayward condition. May our discernment be rooted in and sponsored by the nature of Jesus Christ, the infilling of the Holy Spirit and the precise directives of the Word of God.

Points to Ponder

1. Think of a mistake you made recently. How would you feel if you knew someone was judg-

ing you for what you had done? How would
your feelings change if you knew that same person was viewing your error with genuine concern
and discernment?

2. Write out your guidelines for determining the
   difference between judgment and discernment.
   How will that affect your outlook tomorrow?

Professional Bloodsuckers

*You cannot help people permanently by doing for
them what they could and should do for themselves.*
—William J. H. Boetcker

Bloodsuckers: People who continually sabotage
present circumstances because of past memories or future expectations.

Helplessly weak, bloodsuckers are fixated on
blaming others and justifying themselves when life
dumps on them. They are self-pitying individuals who
tend to live their lives as professional victims. Things
"happen" to them all the time. Their goal is to manipulate and demand the full attention of the caregivers to
whom they are drawn. If allowed, they will ultimately
suck anyone's time, energy and patience. They are, in
short, emotional leeches.

I just bet you can think of someone who fits that
description. In all our talk of wolves, serpents and
swine, you may want to know how to effectively handle the emotional leech. Almost every business, church

or family system will be confronted by a bloodsucker at some time or another.

Just a warning before we get started: If you allow a bloodsucker to "hook" you, you will be taken on an emotional roller coaster ride you'll never forget. If and when you do not fulfill all demands, he or she will rake you over the coals in a heart-rending manner. That's a guarantee. The once weak, pitiful bloodsucker will suddenly become extremely powerful as rage is spewed in your direction.

In your dealings with bloodsuckers, it is important to look beyond the fault and see the need. The art of "bloodsucking" is learned behavior. As children, bloodsuckers were confronted by continual disillusionment, traumatic events (e.g., sexual or physical abuse), Hitler-type control, secrecy or unhealthy dependency. To cope with these experiences, they learned to manipulate themselves and others. These manipulative techniques have become old friends and are hard to give up. For them, such behavior has become as natural as breathing.

Although chronologically and physically bloodsuckers have become adults, they often are locked into an emotional age somewhere between nine and thirteen years. Try to remember your emotional state when you were eleven and you will begin to understand the childish, illogical set of rules bloodsuckers live by.

At first they may have thought Christianity would change everything, but bloodsucking is their only reality. They know no other way of coping.

Those of us in Christian work are often drawn to bloodsuckers because of our desire to help people in need. Our ministry may be as attractive as a warm, glowing fireplace on a blustery winter day to someone going through hard times.

Most of us who are in people-helping professions struggle, at times, with a "Messiah Complex." It feels so good to be needed. We are wired to rescue those assailed by the crashing waves of life. If we're not careful, though, we can play right into the manipulative hand of a bloodsucker because of our own overwhelming need to be needed.

A Lesson From Susie

"Everyone else I have talked to has ultimately abandoned me," she began, her eyes looking pitifully into my own. "I have been to pastors and counselors. They all start out being so loving and kind, but within weeks they don't want to see or hear from me anymore. I just don't know where to turn. I'm at the end of my rope. Today you preached about the unconditional love of God. You seem to be so nice, Pastor Freeman." She paused for a moment, looking very sad and alone. "I need help and I need it bad," she finally said. "Will you help me? I know that *you* won't abandon me."

There I was—a sitting duck, a turkey ready to be plucked, a steer ready for the slaughterhouse. I had no more than three wet-behind-the-ears years of pastoring under my belt when I was confronted by the pleading eyes of a damsel in distress I'll call Susie. My "Messiah Complex" automatically kicked into high gear. Little did I know that Susie was a professional bloodsucker.

My ego was stroked. *What impeccable taste she has. Other counselors have tried and failed. She must see some incredible depth of wisdom and knowledge in me that the others obviously didn't possess. Joel Freeman to the rescue!*

I was set up for the long haul. *The other counselors*

got tired of her. I won't abandon her. No way. I have the power of an endless life in Jesus Christ. There is nothing she could do or say that could make me want to get rid of her.

There was a sense of urgency. *She said she was at the end of her rope. This sounds serious. What could it mean? Suicide? She definitely needs help, and I'll do all I can to help her.*

"Of course I'll help, Susie," I responded enthusiastically. "My wife and I would love to be of service to you at any hour—day or night. And don't worry. I'll stick with you through thick and thin. I'll *never* abandon you," I emphasized with a smile. I gave her our home phone number and a reassuring hug.

You guessed it already. Susie began to call at *all* hours, just as I had offered. Two o'clock in the morning. Eleven-thirty at night. Twelve noon. Her verbal skills were awesome. She could talk like a windstorm with gusts up to fifty miles per hour!

By the third day I was exhausted, but I refused to let Susie know. Laurie had talked to Susie several times and was drained. She decided to pull herself out of the process. Wise woman.

Susie was in debt. She couldn't hold down a job. At twenty-six years of age, she was still living at home, enmeshed in a strange, love-hate relationship with her mother. Men were on her hit-list. She would panic whenever she sensed disapproval in my voice. She felt guilty about everything.

Every helpful strategy I could think of was shot down by her lame excuses and circular reasoning. By the fifth day I was definitely on edge with her. I snapped when the phone rang at 3:15 that morning. I was grumpy, tired and tactless.

"Susie," I said after listening to her ramble on for a

few minutes about a weird dream she had just had with Adolph Hitler playing a piano, "this stuff can wait until a decent hour of the day. You can stay up as late as you want and sleep whenever you want. I don't have that luxury. I have responsibilities with my family and the church. I am tired and need my sleep. Call me tomorrow. Goodbye!"

With that I slammed the phone down in its cradle, unplugged the cord from the wall and groped my way back to bed. Even with the adrenalin pumping I was able to fall off to sleep rather quickly.

Susie was steamed. You could have fried an egg on her head. When she finally got hold of me, I knew it. She lit into me with an intense case of verbal assault and battery.

"Joel Freeman, who do you think you are?" she stormed. "What kind of Christian are you? You promised me that you would *never* abandon me. But you're just like all the rest—a hypocrite. I should have known better. You talk a good show, but when it comes right down to it, you're just interested in yourself and your own little world. And I really thought you were going to be able to help me."

While she talked, a dozen emotions gurgled to the surface, ranging from anger to guilt to feeling defensive. She was an expert, and I was putty in her hands.

Understanding the "Susies" in Our Lives

Six years and a few "Susies" later, I came across some information that has helped me untangle the emotionally damaging counseling situations to which I had been repeatedly contributing. A little older and wiser, I was able to gain some insights and then apply them to my everyday experiences when dealing with people suffering from needs—legitimate or otherwise.

In *Born to Win*, authors Muriel James and Dorothy Jongeward say that children learn how to play roles as they watch their parents and other authority figures cope with the realities of life. According to James and Jongeward:

> As children grow they learn to play parts—heroes, heroines, villains, victims and rescuers. . . . When grown up, people play out their scripts within the context of the society in which they live and which has its own dramatic patterns. As Shakespeare said, "All the world's a stage."[1]

Although I do not believe in the whole transactional analysis behavior model detailed in *Born to Win*, the book provides some interesting concepts worth noting in regard to dealing with people:

> Manipulative roles are part of the rackets and games that contribute to a person's script. A person may play a game in imitation of parental behavior. However, games are usually played by the Child ego state. The Child initiates the game, intending to hook the Child or Parent in other players. The manipulative roles are used to provoke or invite others to respond in specific ways, thus reinforcing the Child's early psychological positions.
>
> On life's many stages it is not uncommon for the entire cast of characters to know how to play all the hands in all the games. Each is able to switch and play three basic roles: Victim, Persecutor, and Rescuer.[2]

I think of it this way: A *Rescuer* is one who creates an unhealthy dependence by going more than 50 percent of the way in helping a *Victim* (Bloodsucker). The *Victim* knows how to invite and then pull the *Rescuer* over the 50 percent line. Before long, the *Rescuer* is doing 70, 80 or 90 percent of the work in the relationship. This harms both people involved.

The Victim is harmed because he or she is encouraged to be continually needy. It is like covering for an alcoholic by repeatedly bailing him out of jail and/or paying his bills. Sooner or later, the Victim needs to become responsible.

The Rescuer is being harmed because his excessive need to be needed is being fed. He thinks that he is helping the Victim when, in fact, he is being used and manipulated to put out another "fire." Time and energy are being sucked from him. If this continues, the Rescuer will become a burned-out, jaded caregiver with misplaced priorities and a jaundiced view.

The Dynamics of a Victim/Rescuer Relationship

Stephen Karpman designed a diagram that aptly illustrates what may happen when a Rescuer crosses the 50 percent line and says, in effect, "You're weak. I'm strong. You're needy. You just sit back and I'll do all I can to try to help you." Karpman calls it the Drama Triangle.

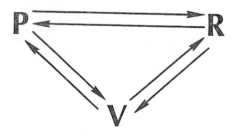

Karpman writes:

> Only three roles are necessary in drama analysis to depict the emotional reversals that are drama. These action roles . . . are the Persecutor, Rescuer, and Victim, or P,R, and V, in the diagram. Drama begins when these roles are established, or are anticipated by the audience. There is no drama unless there is a switch in the roles. . . . [In Games] there is one major switch, i.e., in "I'm Only Trying to Help You" there is one rotation in the drama triangle: The Victim switches to Persecutor and the Rescuer becomes the Victim.[3]

This is exactly what happened in my experience with Susie. Over the years, she had manipulated a number of people to "kick her." The stage had been set for me to come on the scene. I got into the act trying to effect a rescue.

By the fifth day of the rescue, I felt impotent and drained. I realized that I had allowed myself, for whatever reason, to be drawn into an unrealistic rescue. When my many valiant attempts to help were rejected, I moved over to the Victim spot, feeling persecuted and kicked. I had memorized my lines well: "I was only trying to help! Look at all I have done for you. Don't you appreciate me?"

At the same time, Susie moved over to the Persecutor spot as she berated me for my unChristian temper at 3:15 in the morning. She dumped a huge dose of guilt, shame and criticism on me. I accepted all of it and more.

We switched roles one more time as I persecuted her for persecuting me. But in her mind I was just another example of how men have abandoned her. Freeman "stock" was not very valuable from Susie's perspective.

At this point, I want to take a step back and say that I have profound respect for what the Susies of the world go through. All of this talk about Bloodsuckers, Persecutors and Victims can quickly take on a rather harsh, clinical tone. In no way do I wish to minimize her or anyone else's pain.

All of us have experienced the role of the Victim/Bloodsucker. There are times in everyone's life when the bottom falls out. But there is a difference between that and the way that some people are self-pitying and continually shift the responsibility for an unsatisfactory life onto others. Do these lines sound familiar?

"If only I had married someone else . . . "

"When my ship comes in . . . "

"What if I lose my job?"

You could visit some people ten years from now and they would still be grinding the same axe.

We are in a long distance race, not a heated display of quickness and talent in a hundred-yard dash. We must identify our priorities and then pace ourselves appropriately. Starting a race is vital, but ending it well is even more significant. I want to end my "race" with dignity and character.

Steps to Dealing With a Susie

When I met Susie, I got sucked into a trap that she probably wasn't even conscious she was setting. I was not emotionally mature enough to determine what was happening either. She *hooked* me, but more importantly, I was *hookable*. I have had to confront that "Messiah Complex" issue in my life on numerous occasions.

If I could redo that whole situation over again, I would still love Susie and do what I could to help her.

But I would *set definite boundaries*. I would not give her permission to call my house at all hours of the day or night. I am not a crisis hotline counselor. There are plenty of people who have received a sovereign call from God and some fine-tuned training in that area. I have my limits. I cannot and will not do everything for people in need. That's reality.

Also, I would *refer her to a Christ-centered support group* or to a biblically-based counselor. I would give her the phone numbers, but would not make the calls for her. My therapeutic strategy for her would be to give her the tools to stand on her own two feet. If she were passive or outright reactionary about taking advantage of those tools, I would then back off. If she won't make a couple of phone calls, it's obvious the security of being needy outweighs the pain of her condition. When that changes, she'll make the calls.

When pulling back, I would *not allow her to make me feel guilty*. I would gently invite her to accept responsibility for her life and her decisions, pray with her, assure her of my genuine desire to help in the future, and then move on to the next priority for the day.

Was Susie a wolf or swine? Not likely. As I look back, I think she was probably a borderline psychotic sheep. She experienced hallucinations and other types of behavior that make me suspect that diagnosis. She required a professional, caring support system that could provide the personal attention and structure that could handle an energetic bloodsucker like her.

Just one more question. Wasn't Jesus crossing that 50 percent line when he left the ninety-nine sheep in the fold to rescue the one sheep caught in the bushes?

I'll answer it this way: Knowing all these bright ideas about Rescuers, Victims and Persecutors doesn't exempt us from the call of God to reach out to people in need. Only now, when do go after that proverbial one lost sheep, we are more conscious of the internal and external motivating factors. Every time I cross that 50 percent line with someone in need, I actually say to myself, "Freeman, you're crossing that line."

If that one sheep knows how to create the kinds of crises designed to manipulate your sustained attention, you'd better be aware of the dynamics of the transaction. If you aren't, you'll be running from one blaze to the next like an over-worked volunteer fireman. You will become exhausted with the demands of professional bloodsuckers and will have little time or creative energy left for others.

It has been said that if you feed someone a fish, you feed that person for a day. But if you teach that person how to fish, he or she is fed for a lifetime. That's pithy advice for those of us who struggle with "Messiah Complexes." Some people are addicted to working hard for the Lord. I love working hard, but I'd like for my work to be smart.

Points to Ponder

1. Think about the Victim/Persecutor/Rescuer roles described in this chapter. Which would you have related to most when you were eleven years old? What about now? What does that say about your character?

2. How have you historically dealt with the "Susies" in your life? Do you see any need to make a change?

*A positive, from-the-position-
of-strength way to deal
with spiritual germs*

17

Germ Warfare

*Only kisses and money could be so full
of germs and still be popular.*
—Bert Bacharach

Howard Hughes. What does this name remind you of? Celebrated movie producer. Well-known businessman. Billionaire. Famous aviator. Numerous awards. And, of course, a confident-looking man standing in front of the wooden Spruce Goose.

All his achievements are over-shadowed, though, by a hastily taken snapshot of him in his waning years. It's a photo of an eccentric, emaciated man with terror in his eyes. The obsessive-compulsive disorder had taken control: repeated hand-washings after touching a door knob, floor tiles sterilized and cleansed with a toothbrush, plastic gloves, plastic bonnets, plastic coverings all over the place.

Old Howard had every right to be alarmed. Germs are everywhere! I heard that almost every time we wash our hands with soap and water, approximately five million of those disease-producing microorganisms get sluiced down the drain.

As I sit here at my writing desk, I just caught myself chewing the end of my pen. (Kids, don't try this at home.) Oops! I think I just sucked 175,000 germs into my system, and who knows where this pen has been! Yuck!

One could easily become paranoid about the microscopic world of germs. Yet we've got a weapon to combat their assault: the immune system. A person who knows how bad germs are but has little knowledge of the defense mechanisms built into the human body will lead an unbalanced life. He'll live in paranoia of germs.

In order to enjoy life in a balanced manner, a person needs to have some understanding of the way God designed the defense system in the blood to fight germs. We'll take a look at how our defense system works and then use that as an illustration of the defense system Christ has given the church to protect itself from deadly "germs."

Our Ingenious Immune System

Pour a quart of blood into a glass flask and wait to see what happens. Within a relatively short period of time, three distinct bands emerge before your eyes. The thin, yellow layer at the top of the flask is plasma. Platelets and white blood cells make up the pale grey band in the middle. At the bottom lie dark red clumps, the red blood cells. In a drop of blood there would be five million reds, seven thousand whites and three hundred thousand platelets.[1]

In *In His Image*,[2] Phil Yancey does a masterful job

of explaining the purpose of these three main components of the blood in helping fight disease. I'm indebted to his insights.

Red Blood Cells

The reds contain hemoglobin, an iron compound that has an affinity for oxygen. These amazing little fellows carry the oxygen to every cell in the body and clean up the garbage (gases and worn out chemicals) at the same time. An average red endures the cycle of loading, unloading, getting scrubbed by the kidneys and jostling back through the body for about half a million round trips (approximately four months). One billion reds die and are replaced on a daily basis. Parts of them are used in making hair follicles and taste buds.

Platelets

With an average life-span of six to twelve days, platelets play a crucial role in the life-saving process of blood clotting. Let's say you cut your index finger. Immediately, tiny platelets melt like snowflakes and spin a web at the entrance of the wound. Red blood cells are trapped by the web and crash into each other like cars. Soon the build up is thick enough to stop the loss of blood. But there is an extremely small margin for error. Too little clotting and the cut on your finger could prove fatal. Too much clotting and you could ultimately experience a stroke or coronary thrombosis.

White Blood Cells

The fifty billion whites in the bloodstream have a back-up force one hundred times as large in the bone marrow. The blood count of whites doubles and triples when infection occurs anywhere in the body.

Go ahead, try an experiment. Prick your finger.

While the platelets and reds do their clotting, the muscle cells start to swell. Germs invade the site, which makes the whites mad. They rush in with their strange power to engulf and kill those disease-carrying enemies. The awful looking yellowish-green pus that results is actually the graveyard of millions of dead heroes and partly digested germs. In the end, the battlefield is cleansed and new tissue is reconstructed. Infection is quelled once again and you are happy because your finger is like new. Three cheers for white blood cells!

Know the Enemy

You may ask, "What does all of this stuff about blood cells, platelets and germs have to do with the subject of discernment?" So glad you asked. Not long ago I came across a few pages of information titled: "Insights From the World of 'Opportunistic' Germs on How to Protect the Body of Christ."[3] The fine folks at the Institute of Basic Life Principles have graciously allowed me to quote freely from that material. I think you'll find it helpful.

Remember the apostle Paul's final instructions to the leaders of the Ephesian church? Let's reflect on his words:

> Take heed therefore unto yourselves, and to all the flock, over which the Holy Ghost hath made you overseers, to feed the church of God, which He hath purchased with His own blood. For I know this that after my departing shall grievous wolves enter in among you, not sparing the flock (Acts 20:28,29).

The savage wolves which Paul warned about in this passage were also identified by Christ as the same type of "wolves in sheep's clothing" (Matthew 7:15).

These wolves were false prophets and teachers who wanted to ravage the early church. These wolves are among us today. They can be intimidating. They can strike fear in the heart of the most sincere believer. Wolves thrive on that fear.

False prophets and teachers who attack the body of Christ are similar in nature and operation to opportunistic germs which attack the physical body. These germs are disease-carrying organisms. As long as the body's cells are strong, well-nourished and cleansed, opportunistic germs are ineffective.

However, if the body becomes weak or is overly exposed to these microscopic agents, germs will quickly multiply and bring destruction to the body. Let's take a closer look at three types of germs that will provide good illustrations to help us understand the type of warfare we'll be facing in the spiritual realm.

1. "Opportunistic" Viruses (False Prophets)

For I know this that after my departing shall grievous wolves enter in among you, not sparing the flock (Acts 20:29).

Viruses consist of a "genetic message" (nucleic acid) surrounded by a protein coat. When a virus approaches an individual cell in the body, it first "knocks on the door" by means of a precise chemical message. The message is perfect. It can be understood without vagueness or ambiguity. The message is, in effect, "I am here. May I come in?"

If the cell is strong, it will reject the virus and the message of the virus is then rendered void. However, if the cell is weak, it will be "receptive" to the message and allow the virus to gain entrance. In some cases, the cell actually enfolds the virus as a welcome "guest."

The virus is literally gulped into the cell as though it were vacuumed inward through a revolving door.

The virus deceives the cell by appearing to be one of its own kind. In this way, it is precisely like a wolf in sheep's clothing. The cell can't distinguish the message of the virus from the true message within itself.

Having used deception to get into the cell, the virus now uses subversion to carry out its deadly work. This process begins with a second genetic message: "Will you reproduce me? You have taken me in. You have recognized me as your own kind. Perpetuating me is more important than life."

If the cell agrees to reproduce the virus, the message of the virus continues: "Don't trouble yourself by thinking of life. Just relax. I will utilize your 'machinery' and 'resources' for a purpose that is bigger than you are. You are now a part of my purpose and destiny."

Cells were designed by God to reproduce themselves. A virus is incapable of reproducing itself without a host cell. It is totally dependent upon its victims for sustenance. When a virus finds a host cell and begins to rob it of its nutrients, the subversive message says, "You are simply a casualty in a larger battle. This battle is against the ultimate enemy. You are sacrificing your life for me. You can have no greater purpose or fulfillment than this."

One might think that if the cell dies, the virus will die with it and will no longer be a threat to the rest of the body. But it doesn't work that way. The destructive genius of a virus enables it to move to adjacent cells before the infected cell dies. In this way, the disease-producing virus spreads throughout the body.

In the same manner that a cell is tricked into

embracing a virus, so an unsuspecting church can be deceived into accepting a false prophet. This "human virus" will often literally knock on doors to gain support of the membership, one by one. Once false teaching and discord is sown in a congregation, the weeds of gossip and discontent are spread with alarming speed.

Protection Against Viruses

Each cell must be strengthened so it can screen every message that comes to it. Any failure to do so will not only mean the destruction of the cell, but also the infection of the body. Strengthening body cells can only be done by proper nourishment, plenty of fresh water, personal hygiene, sufficient rest and appropriate exercise.

As we have already discovered, when one cell is infected, the white blood cells fight against the virus that has caused the disease. The infected cells must be rescued by other healthy cells. The same method of rescue holds true in the body of Christ.

2. "Opportunistic" Bacteria (False Teachers)

Therefore watch, and remember, that by the space of three years I ceased not to warn every one night and day with tears (Acts 20:31).

Bacteria are single-celled organisms that come into the body in different sizes and shapes: rod-shaped, spherical, curved and spiral. Disease-causing bacteria live and grow in the soft tissues, the blood and the bones. They get their nourishment by digesting blood, muscle or other body tissue. The bacteria's poisonous waste finds its way into the blood stream and causes disease. Some of these diseases are scarlet fever, tetanus, tuberculosis, pneumonia, leprosy, gonorrhea and syphilis.

Bacteria are called opportunistic germs because they wait for favorable conditions in which to grow. A single bacterium can grow and divide into two new cells in less than half an hour. At this rate of multiplication, sixteen million new bacteria are formed in twenty-four hours. At the end of forty-eight hours, there could be billions of bacteria!

It is impossible for the body to keep bacteria out. They are taken into the body through air, food and liquids.

How do bacteria and viruses differ? Viruses enter the body deceptively, whereas disease-producing bacteria are immediately recognized by the body and are attacked. Bacteria are much larger than viruses. In fact, some bacteria contain viruses. And some bacteria are actually beneficial to the body and necessary for the digestion of food. No virus is known to be beneficial.

Just as it is impossible to keep opportunistic germs out of our physical body, so it is impossible to prevent their human counterparts from gaining entry into the church. Every one of us brings bacteria with us wherever we go. Every church is going to have some of these germs. The presence of "bacteria" should be a constant motivation for church leaders to remain spiritually strong and to warn each member to deal properly with the contamination of the world.

"Bacteria" in the church are the complainers and nitpickers who attempt to create division in the body. They will regularly test the strength of church leaders. One indication of the inward strength of a leader is how he responds to criticism. If he wisely responds according to Scripture, the accusers back away. If he reacts in anger, however, the agents know that he is weak and will spring into action.

This test is vividly illustrated in 1 Kings 12:1-19, when Jeroboam challenged Rehoboam's right to be king over Israel. It was 930 B.C. and Solomon's kingdom was in danger of division. Rehoboam rejected the council of his elders and reacted bitterly to the smoldering discontent of the people. Thus, the revolutionary spirit of the northern ten tribes of Israel was fueled by the foolish attitude of Rehoboam.

When a leader successfully responds to reactions and divisions, he confirms his leadership position within the church and strengthens the confidence of the people in the message that he teaches:

> There must be also heresies [divisions and factions] among you, that they which are approved [have handled the test in a spiritually mature, discerning manner] may be made manifest [known] among you (1 Corinthians 11:19).

Getting Rid of Harmful Bacteria

The first line of defense against bacteria is a regular program of purification. This involves removing as many harmful bacteria as possible from the air we breathe, the water we drink and the food we eat. This purification also involves cleansing the body and properly treating all wounds.

The body's second line of defense is its white blood cells. Normally one white cell can overcome fourteen invading bacteria. If the body becomes weakened through improper food, however, a white cell may only be able to attack one bacterium or none at all.

Within the context of the local church, a balanced teaching of the Word of God tends to keep the body pure. People who function like spiritual "bacteria" don't like to hang around where people are filled with discernment from the Word.

3. "Opportunistic" Parasites (Slothful People)

And now, brethren, I commend you to God, and to the word of his grace, which is able to build you up, and to give you an inheritance among all them which are sanctified. I have coveted no man's silver or gold, or apparel. Yea, ye yourselves know that these hands have ministered unto my necessities, and to them that were with me. I have showed you all things, how that so laboring ye ought to support the weak, and to remember the words of the Lord Jesus, how he said, It is more blessed to give than to receive (Acts 20:32-35).

A parasite lives at the expense of the host's nourishment. Some parasites are relatively harmless because they consume only small amounts of the host's food. Other parasites, however, inflict the body with serious pain and possible death.

Christians can simulate a parasite by living in the nourishment of biblical teaching without allowing its truth to be reproduced in their lives. Here's a common occurrence in our churches today: Believers have lots of knowledge stuffed between their ears but no hands or feet to their theology.

Destructive parasites are vain talkers and deceivers, and they "subvert whole houses, teaching things which they ought not, for filthy lucre's sake" (Titus 1:10,11).

The Church's Response to Parasites

To rid the church of parasites, clear instruction from God's Word must be given to the entire body of believers. Only this scriptural medicine will inflict enough discomfort to dislodge any parasites. His Word afflicts believers with the responsibility to be uncontentious, to stay pure, to be industrious and to mind their own business.

Those parasites remaining in the church should be instructed to correct their behavior. They must be sharply rebuked "that they may be sound in the faith" (Titus 1:13). Notice the direction Paul takes as he writes to the Thessalonian Christians:

> In the name of the Lord Jesus Christ, we command you, brothers, to keep away from every brother who is idle and does not live according to the teaching you received from us. For you yourselves know you ought to follow our example. We were not idle when we were with you, nor did we eat anyone's food without paying for it. On the contrary, we worked day and night, laboring and toiling so that we would not be a burden to any of you. We did this, not because we do not have the right to such help, but in order to make ourselves a model for you to follow. For even when we were with you, we gave you this rule: "If a man will not work, he shall not eat." We hear that some among you are idle. They are not busy; they are busybodies. Such people we command and urge in the Lord Jesus Christ to settle down and earn the bread they eat. And as for you, brothers, never tire of doing what is right. If anyone does not obey our instruction in this letter, take special note of him. Do not associate with him, in order that he may feel ashamed. Yet do not regard him as an enemy, but warn him as a brother (2 Thessalonians 3:6-15, NIV).

Keepin Our Defense System in Top Shape

Are you feeling a wee bit like the late Howard Hughes with regards to germs? I hope not.

It is true, germs are everywhere. To combat them physically, we need plenty of rest, a balanced diet, lots of liquids and proper exercise. Even so, germs will still exist in and around a person's body. While we can't isolate ourselves completely from germs, we can have strong bodies that are able to deal with any strategy germs might use to weaken the system. Thank God for white blood cells on the warpath!

Spiritually, the same is true. People who behave like viruses, bacteria or parasites will always be with us. This is not a fatalistic view, merely reality. None of us can arrogantly take high moral ground here. Simply put, we all carry mental, emotional and spiritual "germs." It has been said, "If you're looking for a perfect church, don't join it, because you'll surely mess it up."

There is the very real need to deal with some individuals who are *committed* to behaving like bacteria, viruses or parasites. It is sobering to think that some are out to destroy the church. After a few interactions with an opportunistic germ-like person, you soon discover that he is unreasonable and seems to be comfortable with contradictory thinking.

When such people see others working together in spiritual harmony, it sparks a curious response from them. They don't seem to be satisfied until they have created some sort of discord. It's like waving a red flag in front of a bull. Those committed to functioning like bad germs live with a divided heart darkened and influenced by Satan's kingdom. They are not content until their external environment matches the division they experience in their internal world. They hate the unity that flows from the cross of Jesus Christ.

Banktellers are trained to spot counterfeit money in an odd manner. I am told that 99 percent of their training is with *real* money. They touch it, handle it and study it carefully. When the fake money comes across their desk, it sticks out like a sore thumb.

Those of us in spiritual leadership must remain strong through the highly personal disciplines of prayer, fasting, meditation on Scripture and private worship of Jesus. We train our people in that which is real: Real power in the Holy Spirit. Real resurrection life in Jesus. Real creative vision in God. Real transformation in the Word. Real passion to see lost souls saved. Real love for those in our sphere of influence.

This is the positive, from-the-position-of-strength way to deal with spiritual germs. Periodic reminders regarding the handling of gossip and slander is required so that people can function in an objective, biblical fashion when confronted with diseased statements and attitudes.

Let's keep those white blood cells healthy and on guard, ready to put the double-whammy on germs.

Points to Ponder

1. Do you think you've ever helped someone give your church or workplace a bad case of "spiritual flu"? How can you guard against becoming a carrier of the germs that plant division and discontent?

2. Are you overwhelmed, at times, by "germs" of evil that seem to be everywhere? If so, what can you do to bring balance to your perspective?

Punch Drunk

Apart from God we're weak as water.
—Anonymous

Let's face it. We get so pushed around by the wolves, serpents and swine in this world that sometimes we feel it would just be easier to join them than withstand the abuse. So what can we do when we feel a little dizzy from the repeated blows of life? Read on!

We live in a violent world. Pick up a paper, watch a newscast, check out the latest movie hit—you'll find violence. It's everywhere. Someone said, "I went to a fight and a hockey game broke out." There's no doubt about it: Ice hockey is violent sport.

In fact, there are a number of sports that require excessive amounts of harsh body contact. Carefully observe the swinging elbows and crunching bodies of basketball players as several men go up for a rebound at the same time. And don't forget football. Look at how savagely the ball carrier gets tackled to the ground. Nowhere will you find people so big who can move so fast. Football collisions are violent and spectacular.

I'm reminded of a book by Paul Zimmerman called *A Thinking Man's Guide to Pro Football*. In this fascinating volume, he quotes a physicist's analysis of the impact American football players undergo in a regulation game.[1]

Imagine yourself at a Dallas Cowboys versus Washington Redskins game. You're sitting on the 50-yard line. The ball is snapped . . . the quarterback hands off to his running back . . . he makes a break . . . wham! Incredible! A 250-pound lineman capable of running forty yards in 5.0 seconds collides with a 200-pound running back who is capable of scampering forty yards in just 4.6 seconds. The crowd whoops its approval. The players stagger around momentarily.

According to the physicist, the resultant kinetic energy from the collision of those two particular men running full tilt at each other produces enough force to move an eye-popping thirty-three tons of mass one inch! The impact experienced was one thousand times the force of gravity.

No wonder Joe Namath admits that by age fifty he fully expects to find it hard to walk. Another ex-football great, Merlin Olsen, claims that he has suffered from intense arthritic pain in both knees for a number of years.

Assault and Battery of a Different Nature

Let's leave the football field now and turn a corner to capture a glimpse of the assault and battery Jesus experienced during His earthly visitation. The punishment football players endure is nothing when compared to His pain.

I was first introduced to the extreme manner of Jesus' suffering while reading *The Crucifixion of Jesus* by

C. Truman Davis, M.D. I'd like to share an excerpt with you:

> In the early morning, Jesus, battered and bruised, dehydrated and exhausted from a sleepless night, is taken across Jerusalem to the Praetorium of the Fortress Antonia. . . .
>
> Preparations for the scourging are carried out. The prisoner is stripped of His clothing and His hands tied to a post above His head. The Roman legionnaire steps forward with the flagrum in his hand. This is a short whip consisting of several heavy leather thongs with two small balls of lead attached near the ends of each. The heavy whip is brought down with full force again and again across Jesus' shoulders, back and legs.
>
> At first the heavy thongs cut through the skin only. Then, as the blows continue, they cut deeper into the subcutaneous tissues, producing first an oozing of blood from the capillaries and veins of the skin, and finally spurting arterial bleeding from vessels in the underlying muscles. . . .
>
> Finally the skin of the back is hanging in long ribbons and the entire area is an unrecognizable mass of torn, bleeding tissue. When it is determined by the centurion in charge that the prisoner is near death, the beating is finally stopped.[2]

Our advantage of hindsight permits us to capture the essence of what Isaiah prophesied regarding the Messiah. The ancient prophet declared that the Messiah would be so facially and bodily marred that people would be astonished and hide their faces from Him. The Old Testament seer also said that He would be a man of sorrows, despised by the masses and acquainted with human grief.

How is it that His facial features would be so marred—more than any other man? I discovered the answer when reading Mark's account of the suffering Savior:

> And some began to spit on him, and to cover his face, and to buffet him and to say unto him, "Prophesy": and the servants did strike him with the palms of their hands (Mark 14:65).

Two words leaped out at me when I read this verse in the original Greek language. The first word is *kolaphiz*[3] for the English word *buffet*. It indicates that someone is hammered repeatedly with clenched fists. The specific target of those knock-out punches is the face, which is literally beaten black and blue. Any normal man would have died of a cerebral hemorrhage, football players included.

The second term that indicates their rough handling of Jesus is *rhapisma*[4] which is used for the verb *strike*. This word is used in the plural form revealing a series of blows. Some translations indicate that He was battered with rods rather than with the palms of hands.

The physical trauma intensified when the heavy beam of the cross was tied across His shoulders. The weight of the heavy wooden beam combined with the copious blood loss pushed Him beyond human endurance. We cannot even begin to comprehend the pain He must have experienced as the rough wood gouged into the lacerated skin and muscles of His shoulders.

One Punch Too Many

Just hours prior to this, Christ was in Gethsemane. While we can only speculate here, I am inclined to believe that every foul spirit in hell and on earth was on hand in the garden to pummel the Son of God into submission. Maybe this unrelenting pressure would be the ultimate cause of His premature death. Perhaps the dis-

ciples slept so soundly during this hour of decision because the demonic oppression in the atmosphere was
overwhelming. Perhaps they couldn't help but slumber.
Even after making a third wakeup call, the understanding Master bore no cynicism or sarcasm in His
words, "Rise, let us be going."

Considering this, it doesn't take a rocket scientist
to figure out that we are in a battle on this planet. If our
Master was subjected to satanic attack, should we expect anything less? Without paranoia, I state that at
every turn you and I are lambasted with suggestions
and temptations, some more subtle than others, that are
designed to make us spiritually "punch drunk."

Recently I saw Muhammed Ali, the former boxing
great. It was like watching a movie running in slow motion. Slurred speech. Delayed reaction. He moved like a
man in a drunken stupor. The medical community
theorizes that his condition was brought on by
Parkinson's disease.

Dr. Pacheco, who was Ali's physician for many
years, notes: "Before his last fight with Trevor Berbick
[in the Bahamas, 1981], a CAT scan showed *cavum sep-
tum pellucidum*, damage to the brain."[5]

Could it have been that this man, who had always
lived up to his cocky pre-game predictive rhymes, had
encountered one too many blows to the head? Ali's
brain had been slammed against his cranium on
numerous occasions. Perhaps his brain finally had
given way, reducing the self-proclaimed "Greatest" to
someone almost too painful to watch.

Neil, a friend of mine, reminds me of what happened to Muhammed Ali, but on a different level.
Through the years, I observed Neil sustain repeated
blows from the diabolical one. Each calculated hit had

been designed to further weaken his moral fiber and reduce his spiritual convictions. As weeks turned into months, and months turned into years, the mental torture he had endured culminated to the point where he was emotionally drained. He decided to "give up." A lack of good judgment, wandering eyes and a sprinkling of four-letter words in his vocabulary betrayed his heart's condition.

Plain and simple, Neil was behaving like a fool. Personal pronouns were running rampant. He was increasingly insensitive to the people who cared about him. Defensiveness and fleshly reaction replaced the kind and loving manner which he once had.

Throughout the whole process I was there for him. At times, I must confess, his obnoxious attitudes and deliberate anti-scriptural decisions were almost too much to bear. Those situations tested the mettle of our friendship. He always knew where I stood and yet he couldn't help but discern that I loved him with the unconditional, no-strings-attached love of Jesus.

It was as though Neil had made a deal with the devil: "I'll pull back from following Jesus Christ if you'll stop knocking me around, Satan. I'll do *anything* for just a measure of mental peace and quiet."

The Resource for Fighting Back

I'm thrilled to say that Neil has pulled through as another trophy of God's matchless grace. Once again, the Word of God did not return void. Once again, the Holy Spirit revealed His ability to comfort and convict. Once again, the Father ran toward and passionately embraced another prodigal son.

The resource that came to Neil's aid is manifested in a most unusual passage of Scripture:

And having spoiled principalities and powers, He made a show of them openly, triumphing over them in it (Colossians 2:15).

The Bible is clear about the fact that Satan is the god of this world and that he has an organized host of fallen angels. The key word in this verse is *spoiled*. *Apekdu*[6] paints a graphic picture of Christ's ascension to heaven. Kenneth Wuest and other Greek scholars concur on the point that as Jesus passed through the atmosphere on His way to heaven, demons were on hand to offer planned opposition. Kind of like a demonic gauntlet.

Apekdu stands as a vivid description of Jesus' repulsion of their vicious attack. From this Greek term we see that as Jesus ascended, demons were clutching, clawing and hitting Him. Our glorified Lord literally had to strip them off and push them away from Himself. The evil spirits were endeavoring to keep Him on the earth, hoping to prevent His return to the Father.

Christ's resurrection power is the resource we have available to us. We all get smashed by the enemy. Like a football player who has collided with his opponent at full speed, you feel the force of impact. You stagger about aimlessly for a period of time. The enemy seems to be far too formidable for you. You feel like putty in his hands. He is capable of squashing you and reshaping you at will.

But suddenly, everything stops. The whole scene shifts. Into the arena of your circumstance steps the Champion of champions. He bears scars—the marks of a former conflict. He knows what it is like to be beaten within an inch of His life. He has been pounded like no one else. He understands the desire to give up. He was tempted in all points like you are.

And He is present to give you the eternal perspective:

Being confident of this, that he who began a good work in you will carry it on to completion until the day of Jesus Christ (Philippians 1:6, NIV).

The one who calls you is faithful and he will do it (1 Thessalonians 5:24, NIV).

There's hope. You don't have to accept a fool's lot in life. You can reject the thoughts that claim you are unavoidably becoming a wolf-like person. You are not punch drunk. You are a child of God. You've read the back of The Book. You know that we win!

Points to Ponder

1. What kind of help with our difficulties should we expect from our Champion, who "has been tempted in all things as we are, yet without sin"?

2. Have you sustained repeated blows from Satan, like Neil? What difference has Jesus' resurrection power made in your life?

The Desperation Factor

*The person who is not hungry says that
the coconut has a hard shell.
—African Tribal Saying*

Ever been in a river up to your behind in piranhas? No place for a casual relationship with God. No way! "Bless-the-cat-and-while-You're-at-it-bless-me-real-good" prayers don't cut it during times of intense encounters with eternal reality.

Sure, I know life isn't always on-the-edge-of-your-seat living. In the movies, Tarzan isn't swinging from vines *every* minute. He has quiet, uninspiring moments with Jane and Cheetah. Superman isn't ducking into *every* telephone booth he sees. Sometimes he just sits there looking at Lois through his nerdy glasses. There are times when life beckons us to throw our brains in neutral while lounging in a porch swing, sipping ice-cold lemonade.

Yet, there is the clarion call to be an on-fire, God-fearing, Bible-loving, sin-hating, devil-thumping,

Spirit-filled Christian. Anything less and we're inoculated with just enough Christianity to be miserable.

A Word of Desperation

"O!"—this tiny word in the Bible reveals how important it is to be continually desperate for God. It's used about a thousand times in the Scriptures. The writers of Psalms use it on 396 different occasions, punctuating their emotional pain with a screaming exclamation point.

"O!"

"O God!"

"O God of Abraham, Isaac and Jacob!"

"O God of Abraham, Isaac and Jacob, help me!"

"O God of Abraham, Isaac and Jacob, help me right now!"

Sound familiar? "O!" initiates an anguished plea for help. A little name-dropping along the way doesn't hurt either.

If you've ever used "O!", you're in good company.

"O Lord God!" Gideon is fearing for his very life. He has just seen the angel of the Lord face to face!

"O God!" Can you hear Jacob's distress? He is about to meet Esau for the first time since stealing his birthright some twenty years prior.

"O Lord, what shall I say?" After the miraculous defeat of Jericho, Israel has lost thirty-six men in a skirmish at Ai and Joshua needs some wisdom from above.

None of these "O!"s are followed by monotone, grocery-list petitions. We could call it crisis praying. Pleading. Sincerity. Anguish. Urgency. We could call it the desperation factor.

Considering the opposition we talked about in this book, we may be tempted to say, "O No!" Surrounded by evil, we are tempted to feel overwhelmed.

It is easy to adopt a mindset suspicious of evil tendencies in everything and everyone. We can expend a lot of time and energy fighting evil people and evil circumstances. I have seen so many people get caught up in a cause at the expense of getting to know the person of Christ. They generate a lot of heat but very little light.

Seeing With Spiritual Eyes

The desperation for God I am talking about is our passion for purity: "Blessed are the pure in heart, for they will see God" (Matthew 5:8). That is the core of the matter—seeing God with our spiritual eyes. How does it work?

Let's say you are confronted by a person who exhibits an advanced stage of wolfish behavior. What can you do? You are a feisty individual. No head-in-the-sand stuff for you. No sir. You are discerning the kingdom issues at hand.

By keeping short accounts with the Holy Spirit, you maintain your clear view of Jesus. With a tender heart, you are sensitive to His every suggestion. You diligently avoid locking your focus on the fool's behavior. You're too busy gazing at the One who is the hope of glory. With specific instructions from the Word, in the power of the Spirit, you hit the powers of darkness head-on.

Building your foundation in the Word of God, you are learning to obey the impressions of the Holy Spirit. You are led by the Spirit to be extremely patient with a number of individuals who don't seem to deserve it.

With others you are cautioned by the Spirit. You are careful. You approach them in a both-eyes-and-both-ears-open state of alertness. Not always able to immediately understand why, you remain guarded. Sooner or later your discernment is verified. In all this you retain a generous spirit, a loving heart and a sometimes wild and crazy sense of humor.

Each situation is different. There isn't a *Ten Steps to Happy Wolf Handling* manual you can refer to. It is a spiritual battle requiring warriors who are in desperate need of God.

Take a Look at the Big Picture

If you have been victimized by wolf-type people, may I say something to you? You'll always be able to recall the events, but with Christ' help you can let the bitterness go. Learn to risk again. Life is too short to be bound by the shackles of suspicion and fear.

I am reminded of a poignant story told by my friend, Herscheld Martin. Herscheld grew up in a poor family in the South during The Great Depression of the 1930s. As a young lad he was continually amazed by the number of hobos who, after tumbling off the nearby trains, found their way to his house on the edge of town.

The hobos were always greeted with a warm meal, a smile and some lodging. Curiosity finally got the best of Herscheld. One day he asked a particularly friendly tramp why he and his kind always came to his house. The traveling man took young Herscheld by the hand and led him out to the street, pointing to a black mark etched on the curb in front of the house.

"See that?" he asked. "Your house has been marked. That is the signal for every hobo passing through the area that your family will provide food and shelter." The next day, Herscheld took his mother out to the street to show her the mark, explaining its long-term implications. He offered to wash the mark off the curb.

She turned to him with tears in her eyes, putting her hand on his shoulder. "Son," she responded, "I don't want you to wash it off. I have known about the mark all along. Let's keep it there and serve as many needy people as we possibly can. God is faithful."

Mrs. Martin was a discerning woman. She knew what was happening. Probably many people took advantage of her hospitality. But she saw the bigger picture instead of the mark on the curb. She saw eternal value. She saw God and He was her audience. He was the one she was serving.

I cannot give principles for obtaining and retaining a tender heart. I can only recommend that we cry out to God. Let's be desperate for Him. You may want to do a Bible study on the power-packed "O!" It may prime the pump.

It's only as we look to Him that He will give us the discernment to deal with the wolves, swine and serpents in our lives. He also will keep us from becoming wolves ourselves.

Points to Ponder

1. Desperation is usually considered a sign of weakness. Scripture makes it clear, however, that being "desperate" for God is the sure way to find strength. How can this be?

2. What is the most important principle you have gleaned from this book? How does it apply to your everyday life?

Afterword

After reading this book, if you have not made your peace with God, there is one thing that is necessary. This one thing is more necessary than your next breath, because you are only one heartbeat away from death. Having this one thing is more important than having contentment, self-control, answers to all your "why" questions, or relief from all the pain and suffering you may be experiencing at this present time. If you do not have this one thing, even what you seem to have will be taken away for all eternity.

I am talking about the gift of God. Consider His gift. He gave Himself in the person of His Son. *This one thing* is your personal acceptance of God's gift—Jesus Christ.

God's compassion compelled Him to build a bridge of reconciliation to all people without regard to cost. He did not spare His own Son, Jesus Christ, who humbly took the form of a man about 2,000 years ago and satisfied every demand of perfection God required. Then, in order to satisfy the justice of God, the sins of all of us were laid on Christ so we would not have to suffer the eternal consequences of our sins.

Jesus voluntarily suffered horrible anguish for us by being nailed to a wooden cross and dying in our place. He was buried, rose again the third day and ascended into heaven, representing the whole world with His precious blood.

He has forgiven your sins. In fact, there is nothing about your past that shocks Him. He has provided meaning for the emotional agony you have endured in your lifetime. He has exhibited His genuine friendship by dying for you, in your place, with no strings attached.

There is nothing more important than being honest about your need to receive the free gift of eternal life. To do this, invite Jesus to come and live inside your heart. The issue is not what you can do to earn God's favor, but what He has already done for you in expressing His unconditional love to you.

Come to Him right now, just as you are, by simple faith and pray:

Dear God, I thank you for sending Your Son, Jesus, to die on the cross in my place for my sins. I now accept the fact that the shed blood of Jesus has cleansed me from all unrighteousness. I receive Jesus Christ into my heart as the Lord of my life. I want to live for Him for the rest of my life. Thank you for accepting me just as I am. In Jesus' name. Amen.

If you prayed this prayer, please feel free to contact me for some helpful information about your new life in Christ. Enclose a self-addressed, stamped envelope and send it to: 5110 Frederick Avenue, Baltimore, MD, 21229.

Fool's Gold

A study of the Scriptures will aid our understanding about the subject of fools. There are five main types of fools mentioned in the Hebrew language of the Old Testament:

1. SIMPLE FOOL (pethîy)

Psalm 19:7: The law of the Lord is perfect, converting the soul: the testimony of the Lord is sure, making wise the *simple*.

Psalm 116:6: The Lord preserveth the *simple*: I was brought low, and he helped me.

Psalm 119:130: The entrance of thy words giveth light; it giveth understanding unto the *simple*.

Proverbs 1:4: To give subtilty to the *simple*, to the young man knowledge and discretion.

Proverbs 1:22: How long, ye *simple* ones, will ye love *simplicity*? and the scorners delight in their scorning, and fools hate knowledge?

Proverbs 1:32: For the turning away of the *simple* shall slay them, and the prosperity of fools shall destroy them.

Proverbs 7:7: And beheld among the *simple* ones, I discerned among the youths, a young man void of understanding.

Proverbs 8:5: O ye *simple*, understand wisdom: and ye fools, be ye of an understanding heart.

Proverbs 9:4-6: Whoso is *simple*, let him turn in hither: as for him that wanteth understanding, she saith to him, Come, eat of my bread, and drink of the wine which I have mingled. Forsake the foolish, and live; and go in the way of understanding.

Proverbs 9:16: Whoso is *simple*, let him turn in hither: and as for him that wanteth understanding, she saith to him.

Proverbs 14:15: The *simple* believeth every word: but the prudent man looketh well to his going.

Proverbs 14:18: The *simple* inherit folly: but the prudent are crowned with knowledge.

Proverbs 19:25: Smite a scorner, and the *simple* will beware: and reprove one that hath understanding, and he will understand knowledge.

Proverbs 22:3: A prudent man foreseeth the evil, and hideth himself: but the *simple* pass on, and are punished.

Proverbs 27:12: A prudent man forseeth the evil, and hideth himself; but the *simple* pass on, and are punished.

2. UNREASONABLE FOOL (evîyl)

Psalm 38:5: My wounds stink and are corrupt because of my *foolishness*.

Psalm 69:5: O God, thou knowest my *foolishness*; and my sins are not hid from thee.

Psalm 107:17: *Fools* because of their transgression, and because of their iniquities, are afflicted.

Proverbs 1:7: The fear of the Lord is the beginning of knowledge: but *fools* despise wisdom and instruction.

Proverbs 5:23: He shall die without instruction; and in the greatness of his *folly* he shall go astray.

Proverbs 7:22: He goeth after her straightway, as an ox goeth to the slaughter, or as a *fool* to the correction of the stocks.

Proverbs 10:8: The wise in heart will receive commandments: but a prating *fool* shall fall.

Proverbs 10:10: He that winketh with the eye causeth sorrow: but a prating *fool* shall fall.

Proverbs 10:21: The lips of the righteous feed many: but *fools* die for want of wisdom.

Proverbs 11:29: He that troubleth his own house shall inherit the wind: and the *fool* shall be servant to the wise of heart.

Proverbs 12:15,16: The way of a *fool* is right in his own eyes: but he that hearkeneth unto counsel is wise. A *fool's* wrath is presently known: but a prudent man covereth shame.

Proverbs 14:3: In the mouth of the *foolish* is a rod of pride: but the lips of the wise shall preserve them.

Proverbs 14:9: *Fools* make a mock at sin: but among the righteous there is favour.

Proverbs 14:29: He that is slow to wrath is of great understanding: but he that is hasty of spirit exalteth *folly*.

Proverbs 15:5: A *fool* despiseth his father's instruction: but he that regardeth reproof is prudent.

Proverbs 15:21: *Folly* is joy to him that is destitute of wisdom: but a man of understanding walketh uprightly.

Proverbs 16:22: Understanding is a well-spring of life unto him that hath it: but the instruction of *fools* is folly.

Proverbs 17:28: Even a *fool* when he holdeth his peace, is counted wise: and he that shutteth his lips is esteemed a man of understanding.

Proverbs 18:13: He that answereth a matter before he heareth it, it is *folly* and shame unto him.

Proverbs 19:3: The *foolishness* of man perverteth his way: and his heart fretteth against the Lord.

Proverbs 20:3: It is an honour for a man to cease from strife: but every *fool* will be meddling.

Proverbs 22:15: *Foolishness* is bound in the heart of a child; but the rod of correction shall drive it far from him.

Proverbs 24:7-9: Wisdom is too high for a *fool*: he openeth not his mouth in the gate. He that deviseth to do evil shall be called a mischievous person. The thought of *foolishness* is sin: and the *scorner* is an abomination to men.

Proverbs 27:3: A stone is heavy, and the sand weighty; but a *fool's* wrath is heavier than them both.

Proverbs 27:22: Though thou shouldest bray a *fool* in a mortar among wheat with a pestle, yet will not his *foolishness* depart from him.

Proverbs 29:9: If a wise man contendeth with a *foolish* man, whether he rage or laugh, there is no rest.

Jeremiah 4:22: For my people is *foolish*, they have not known me; they are sottish children, and they have none understanding: they are wise to do evil, but to do good they have no knowledge.

Zechariah 11:15: And the Lord said unto me, Take unto thee yet the instruments of a *foolish* shepherd.

3. STUBBORN FOOL (kecîyl)

1 Samuel 26:21: Then said Saul, I have sinned: return, my son David: for I will no more do thee harm, because my soul was precious in thine eyes this day: behold, I have played the *fool*, and have erred exceedingly.

Psalm 49:10: For he seeth that wise men die, likewise the *fool* and the brutish person perish, and leave their wealth to others.

Psalm 92:6: A brutish man knoweth not; neither doth a *fool* understand this.

Psalm 94:8: Understand, ye brutish among the people: and ye *fools*, when will ye be wise?

Proverbs 1:22: How long, ye simple ones, will ye love

simplicity? and the scorners delight in their scorning, and *fools* hate knowledge?

Proverbs 1:32: For the turning away of the simple shall slay them, and the prosperity of *fools* shall destroy them.

Proverbs 3:35: The wise shall inherit glory: but shame shall be the promotion of *fools*.

Proverbs 8:5: O ye simple, understand wisdom: and, ye *fools* be ye of an understanding heart.

Proverbs 9:13: A *foolish* woman is clamorous: she is simple, and knoweth nothing.

Proverbs 10:1: The proverbs of Solomon. A wise son maketh a glad father: but a *foolish* son is the heaviness of his mother.

Proverbs 10:18: He that hideth hatred with lying lips, and he that uttereth a slander, is a *fool*.

Proverbs 12:23: A prudent man concealeth knowledge: but the heart of *fools* proclaimeth foolishness.

Proverbs 13:16: Every prudent man dealeth with knowledge: but a *fool* layeth open his folly.

Proverbs 13:19,20: The desire accomplished is sweet to the soul: but it is abomination to *fools* to depart from evil. He that walketh with wise men shall be wise: but a companion of *fools* shall be destroyed.

Proverbs 14:7,8: Go from the presence of a *foolish* man, when thou perceivest not in him the lips of knowledge. The wisdom of the prudent is to understand his way: but the folly of *fools* is deceit.

Proverbs 14:16: A wise man feareth, and departeth from evil: but the *fool* rageth, and is confident.

Proverbs 14:24: The crown of the wise is their riches: but the *foolishness* of *fools* is folly.

Proverbs 14:33: Wisdom resteth in the heart of him that hath understanding: but that which is in the midst of *fools* is made known.

Proverbs 15:2: The tongue of the wise useth knowledge aright: but the mouth of *fools* poureth out foolishness.

Proverbs 15:7: The lips of the wise disperse knowledge: but the heart of the *foolish* doeth not so.

Proverbs 15:14: The heart of him that hath understanding seeketh knowledge: but the mouth of *fools* feedeth on *foolishness*.

Proverbs 15:20: A wise son maketh a glad father: but a *foolish* man despiseth his mother.

Proverbs 17:10: A reproof entereth more into a wise man than an hundred stripes into a *fool*.

Proverbs 17:12: Let a bear robbed of her whelps meet a man, rather than a *fool* in his folly.

Proverbs 17:16: Wherefore is there a price in the hand of a *fool* to get wisdom, seeing he hath no heart to it?

Proverbs 17:21: He that begetteth a *fool* doeth it to his sorrow: and the father of a *fool* hath no joy.

Proverbs 17:24,25: Wisdom is before him that hath understanding; but the eyes of a *fool* are in the ends of the earth. A *foolish* son is a grief to his father, and bitterness to her that bare him.

Proverbs 18:2: A *fool* hath no delight in understanding, but that his heart may discover itself.

Proverbs 18:6,7: A *fool's* lips enter into contention, and his mouth calleth for strokes. A *fool's* mouth is his destruction, and his lips are the snare of his soul.

Proverbs 19:1: Better is the poor that walketh in his integrity, than he that is perverse in his lips, and is a *fool*.

Proverbs 19:10: Delight is not seemly for a *fool*; much less for a servant to have rule over princes.

Proverbs 19:13: A *foolish* son is the calamity of his father: and the contentions of a wife are a continual dropping.

Proverbs 19:29: Judgments are prepared for scorners, and stripes for the back of *fools*.

Proverbs 21:20: There is treasure to be desired and oil in the dwelling of the wise; but a *foolish* man spendeth it up.

Proverbs 23:9: Speak not in the ears of a *fool*: for he will despise the wisdom of thy words.

Proverbs 26:1: As snow in summer, and as rain in harvest, so honour is not seemly for a *fool*.

Proverbs 26:3-9: A whip for the horse, a bridle for the ass, and a rod for the *fool's* back. Answer not a *fool* according to his folly, lest thou also be like unto him. Answer a *fool* according to his folly, lest he be wise in his own conceit. He that sendeth a message by the hand of a *fool* cutteth off the feet, and drinketh damage. The legs of the lame are not equal: so is a parable in the mouth of *fools*. As he that bindeth a stone in a sling, so is he that giveth honour to a *fool*. As a thorn goeth up into the hand of a drunkard, so is a parable in the mouth of *fools*.

Proverbs 26:11,12: As a dog returneth to his vomit, so a *fool* returneth to his folly. Seest thou a man wise in his own conceit? there is more hope of a *fool* than of him.

Proverbs 28:26: He that trusteth in his own heart is a *fool*: but whoso walketh wisely, he shall be delivered.

Proverbs 29:11: A *fool* uttereth all his mind: but a wise man keepeth it in till afterwards.

Proverbs 29:20: Seest thou a man that is hasty in his words? there is more hope of a *fool* than of him.

Ecclesiastes 2:14: The wise man's eyes are in his head; but the *fool* walketh in darkness: and I myself perceived also that one event happeneth to them all.

Ecclesiastes 4:5: The *fool* foldeth his hands together, and eateth his own flesh.

Ecclesiastes 5:3: For a dream cometh through the multitude of business; and a *fool's* voice is known by multitude of words.

Ecclesiastes 7:6: For as the crackling of thorns under a pot, so is the laughter of the *fool*: this also is vanity.

Ecclesiastes 9:17: The words of wise men are heard in quiet more than the cry of him that ruleth among *fools*.

Ecclesiastes 10:12: The words of a wise man's mouth are gracious; but the lips of a *fool* will swallow up himself.

4. MOCKING FOOL (lûwts)

Job 16:20: My friends *scorn* me: but mine eye poureth out tears unto God.

Psalm 1:1: Blessed is the man that walketh not in the counsel of the ungodly, nor standeth in the way of sinners, nor sitteth in the seat of the scornful.

Psalm 22:7: All they that see me laugh me to *scorn*: they shoot out the lip, they shake the head.

Proverbs 1:22: How long, ye simple ones, will ye love simplicity? and the *scorners* delight in their scorning, and fools hate knowledge?

Proverbs 9:7,8: He that reproveth a *scorner* getteth to himself shame: and he that rebuketh a wicked man getteth himself a blot. Reprove not a *scorner*, lest he hate thee: rebuke a wise man, and he will love thee.

Proverbs 9:12: If thou be wise, thou shalt be wise for thyself: but if thou *scornest*, thou alone shalt bear it.

Proverbs 13:1: A wise son heareth his father's instruction: but a *scorner* heareth not rebuke.

Proverbs 14:6: A *scorner* seeketh wisdom, and findeth it not: but knowledge is easy unto him that understandeth.

Proverbs 15:12: A *scorner* loveth not one that reproveth him: neither will he go unto the wise.

Proverbs 19:25: Smite a *scorner*, and the simple will beware: and reprove one that hath understanding, and he will understand knowledge.

Proverbs 19:28,29: An ungodly witness *scorneth* judgment: and the mouth of the wicked devoureth iniquity. Judgments are prepared for *scorners*, and stripes for the back of fools.

Proverbs 21:11: When the *scorner* is punished, the simple is made wise: and when the wise is instructed, he receiveth knowledge.

Proverbs 21:24: A proud and haughty man—"*Scoffer*" is his name: He acts with arrogant pride (TEV).

Proverbs 22:10: Cast out the *scorner*, and contention shall go out; yea, strife and reproach shall cease.

Proverbs 24:9: The thought of foolishness is sin: and the *scorner* is an abomination to men.

Isaiah 29:20: For the terrible one is brought to nought, and the *scorner* is consumed, and all that watch for iniquity are cut off.

5. COMMITTED FOOL (nâbâl)

Genesis 34:7: And the sons of Jacob came out of the field when they heard it: and the men were grieved, and they were very wroth, because he had wrought *folly* in Israel in lying with Jacob's daughter; which thing ought not to be done.

Deuteronomy 32:6: Do ye thus requite the Lord, O *foolish* people and unwise? is not he thy father that hath bought thee? hath he not made thee, and established thee?

Deuteronomy 32:21: They have moved me to jealousy with that which is not God; they have provoked me to anger with their vanities: and I will move them to jealousy with those which are not a people; I will provoke them to anger with a *foolish* nation.

Joshua 7:15: And it shall be, that he that is taken with the accursed thing shall be burnt with fire, he and all that he hath: because he hath transgressed the covenant of the Lord, and because he hath wrought *folly* in Israel.

Judges 19:23: And the man, the master of the house, sent out unto them, and said unto them, Nay, my brethren, nay, I pray you, do not so wickedly; seeing that this man is come into mine house, do not this *folly*.

Judges 20:6: And I took my concubine, and cut her in pieces, and sent her throughout all the country of the inheritance of Israel: for they have committed lewdness and *folly* in Israel.

Judges 20:10: And we will take ten men of an hundred throughout all the tribes of Israel, and an hundred of a thousand, and a thousand out of ten thousand, to fetch victual for the people, that they may do, when they come to Gibeah of Benjamin, according to all the *folly* that they have wrought in Israel.

1 Samuel 25:25: Let not my lord, I pray thee, regard this man of Belial, even Nabal: for as his name is, so is he; Nabal is his name, and *folly* is with him: but I thine handmaid saw not the young men of my lord, whom thou didst send.

2 Samuel 13:12,13: And she answered him, Nay, my brother, do not force me; for no such thing ought to be done in Israel: do not thou this *folly*. And I, whither shall I cause my shame to go? and as for thee, thou shalt be as one of the *fools* in Israel. Now therefore, I pray thee, speak unto the king; for he will not withhold me from thee.

Job 42:8: Therefore take unto you now seven bullocks and seven rams, and go to my servant Job, and offer up for yourselves a burnt-offering; and my servant Job shall pray for you: for him will I accept: lest I deal with you after your *folly*, in that ye have not spoken of me the thing which is right, like my servant Job.

Psalm 14:1: The *fool* hath said in his heart, There is no God. They are corrupt, they have done abominable works, there is none that doeth good.

Psalm 53:1: The *fool* hath said in his heart, There is no God. Corrupt are they, and have done abominable iniquity: there is none that doeth good.

Proverbs 17:7: Excellent speech becometh not a *fool*: much less do lying lips a prince.

Proverbs 17:21: He that begetteth a *fool* doeth it to his sorrow: and the father of a *fool* hath no joy.

Proverbs 30:32: If thou hast done *foolishly* in lifting up thyself, or if thou hast thought evil, lay thine hand upon thy mouth.

Isaiah 9:17: Therefore the Lord shall have no joy in their young men, neither shall have mercy on their fatherless and widows: for every one is an hypocrite and an evil-doer, and every mouth speaketh *folly*. For all this his anger is not turned away, but his hand is stretched out still.

Jeremiah 17:11: As the partridge sitteth on eggs, and hatcheth them not; so he that getteth riches, and not by right, shall leave them in the midst of his days, and at his end shall be a *fool*.

Ezekiel 13:3: Thus saith the Lord GOD; Woe unto the *foolish* prophets, that follow their own spirit, and have seen nothing!

How to Guard Against the Defilement of Listening to an Evil Report

The following material is the most complete, concise study I have ever seen on the subject of listening to an evil report. After reading this, you will have a clear understanding of the sins of the tongue and a scripturally-based strategy for cleansing your mind from defilement. I thank The Institute in Basic Life Principles for granting permission to reprint this valuable work.

THE PROBLEM

- What causes conflicts in families, churches or organizations to flare out of control and split the entire group?
- What causes close friendships to be broken when neither party offended the other?
- Why are attempts to restore a fallen Christian brother or sister often met with defeat?

A MAJOR CAUSE: WRONG RESPONSES TO AN EVIL REPORT

Definition: An evil report involves distortion of facts, incomplete facts or false information. It is given with wrong motivations and causes the hearer to come to inaccurate conclusions and to respond with unscriptural "solutions."

Evil reports are so destructive that they can even destroy long-lasting, close friendships: "A whisperer separateth chief friends" (Proverbs 16:28).

Note: Wrongdoing should never be covered over. It must be brought to the attention of those who are responsible and dealt with in a scriptural manner. This necessary process will be damaged by the defilement of an evil report.

In the medical world, there are stages in the development of a disease. In the same way, there are stages of destruction to a spiritually healthy person.

STAGES OF PHYSICAL DEFILEMENT

1. *Ignorance* of preventive measures to avoid contamination

2. *Exposure* to one who is already infected

3. *Contamination* (defilement) by allowing the germs to enter our system

4. *Infection* as the germs overcome our normal defenses

5. *Disease* when the infection destroys vital life-supporting functions

THE STAGES OF SPIRITUAL DEFILEMENT

1. Ignorance

Satan will gain an advantage over us if we are ignorant of his devices (see 2 Corinthians 2:11).

Ignorance is not being aware of the destructive power of untrue or distorted words.

"The tongue is a fire, a world of iniquity . . . it *defileth* the whole body, and setteth on fire the course of nature; and it is set on fire of hell" (James 3:6).

A. Ignorance of *how words destroy close friendships:*

"He that covereth a transgression seeketh love; but he that repeateth a matter separateth very friends" (Proverbs 17:9).

B. Ignorance of *how the unclean defile the clean*, rather than the clean influencing the unclean (see Haggai 2:11-14).

C. Ignorance of *what constitutes an evil report:*

It is an unauthorized, distorted or false report which influences us to form an evil opinion about another person.

D. Ignorance of *how evil reports are given:*

Evil reports are communicated by words, facial expressions, gestures and tonal patterns. They can be subtle or obvious, quiet or angry, sweet or bitter.

E. Ignorance of *who gives evil reports:*

Giving bad reports is part of the fallen nature of every person.

WHISPERER:	One who secretly or privately passes on evil reports to others (see Psalm 41:7).
GOSSIP:	One who magnifies and sensationalizes rumors and partial information.
SLANDERER:	One who seeks to destroy another's credibility or reputation with damaging facts, distortions of facts or evil suspicions (see Numbers 14:36).
BUSYBODY:	One who digs up evil reports and makes it his business to spread them by means of gossip, slander or whispering. Such an action is as great a sin as murder or stealing. It is classified with these by God when He warns: "Let none of you suffer as a murderer, or as a thief, or as an evildoer, or as a *busybody* in other men's matters" (1 Peter 4:15).

F. Ignorance of *what motivates an evil report* (see James 3:14-18):

BITTERNESS:	Reacting because of personal hurts
REBELLION:	Justifying an independent spirit
DECEPTION:	Believing that evil reports are right to give
PRIDE:	Wanting to exalt self
GUILT:	Justifying past actions or attitudes
ENVY:	Desiring what another has

G. Ignorance of *how susceptible we are to evil reports:*

We enjoy hearing them because they exalt us. They bring down or hurt those whom we dislike.

H. Ignorance of *how Satan uses evil reports:*
 • To discredit spiritual leadership
 • To cause Christians to close their spirits toward each other
 • To multiply conflicts and produce more ungodliness
 • To prompt non-Christians to mock Christianity and reject Christ

2. **Exposure**

"A prudent man forseeth the evil, and hideth himself; but the simple pass on and are punished" (Proverbs 27:12).

Exposure is entering into conversation with a person who is a carrier of an evil report.

• How does God want us to respond?

"Whoso privily slandereth his neighbor, him will I *cut off*" (Psalm 101:5).

"And *have no fellowship* with the unfruitful works of darkness, but rather reprove them. For it is a shame even to speak of those things which are done of them in secret" (Ephesians 5:11,12).

"Now I beseech you, brethren, *mark them* which cause divisions and offenses contrary to the doctrine which ye have learned; and *avoid them*" (Romans 16:17).

• We have protective physical defenses to warn us about

physical contamination. We can smell, see or taste it. Sometimes, however, we are unaware of contamination until it is too late.

* In the same way, God gives us protective spiritual defenses to warn us about spiritual contamination. We can sense the promptings of God's Holy Spirit, follow the warnings of God's Word and obey the wise counsel of our human authorities. Sometimes, however, we are unaware of spiritual danger until it is too late.

A. How to detect a carrier of an evil report:
1. A carrier will usually *test your spirit* before giving you the evil report. Any evidence of a compatible spirit in you will encourage him to give you the report.

2. A carrier will usually *check your acceptance* of his report before giving it to you. He may do this by asking for your opinion about the person or dropping a negative comment and observing your response to it.

3. A carrier will often *get you to ask* for the evil report by creating curiosity for it. Some starters are: "Have you heard about (the person)?" "Wait until I tell you about (the person)!"

4. A carrier may communicate an evil report by *asking us for counsel* or by sharing a concern for the person involved.

5. A carrier may use evil reports to *get you to admire* him or her because of being on the inside and having access to privileged information.

6. A carrier is usually one who *evokes vivid details* of evil and will even search them out. God condemns such "detectives of darkness" whose tongues are like sharp swords.

B. How to detect an evil report:
Five questions to ask *before* listening to a carrier:

1. What is your reason for telling me?

   Widening the circle of gossip only compounds the problem.

2. Where did you get your information?

   Refusal to identify the source of information is a sure signal of an evil report.

3. Have you gone to those directly involved?

   Spirituality is not measured by how well we expose an offender, but by how effectively we restore an offender (see Galatians 6:1).

4. Have you personally checked out all of the facts?

   Even "facts" become distorted when not balanced with other facts or when given with negative motives.

5. Can I quote you if I check this out?

   Those who give evil reports often claim that they are "misquoted." This is because their words and overriding impressions are reported.

3. **Defilement**

"The *words* of a talebearer are as *wounds*, and they go down into the innermost parts of the belly" (Proverbs 26:22).

Defilement is receiving an evil report from another person and believing that it is true.

- In the same way that touching a diseased person will defile one's hands, listening to an evil report will defile one's mind. It is a reality which must be properly dealt with, "lest any root of bitterness springing up trouble you, and thereby *many be defiled*" (Hebrews 12:15).

A classic illustration of many listening to an evil report: Absalom used an innocent sounding evil report to steal the hearts of almost an entire nation and lead a revolt against his own father, King David. The report emphasized his "concern" for suffering people, his "deep desire" that justice be done and his "ability" to be a better administrator than his father. Actually, Absalom was bitter because his father did not bring judgment to Absalom's half-brother for immorality, so he took matters into his own hands and was rejected for it.

And it came to pass after this, that Absalom prepared him chariots and horses, and fifty men to run *before him*.[1]
And Absalom rose up *early*,[2] and stood beside the way of the *gate*;[3] and it was so, that when any man that had a controversy came to the king for *judgment*,[4] then Absalom *called unto him*[5] and said, "Of what city art thou?" And he said, "Thy servant is of one of the tribes of Israel."
And Absalom said unto him, "See, thy matters are *good and right*;[6] but *there is no man deputed of the king to hear thee*." [7]
Absalom said, moreover, "Oh that I were made judge in *the land*,[8] that every man which hath any suit or cause might come *unto me*,[9] and I would do him justice!"
And it was so, that when any man came nigh to him to do him obeisance, he put forth his hand, and took him, and *kissed him*.[10]
. . . So Absalom *stole the hearts*[11] of the men of Israel (2 Samuel 15:1-6).

4. Infection

"The simple believeth every word: but the prudent man looketh well to his going" (Proverbs 14:15).

---

1. He gathered and organized a group that would be loyal to him, rather than to the one whom he served.
2. He was energetic and disciplined.
3. He made himself available to the people.
4. He sought out those who had grievances.
5. He had a personal interest in people.
6. He took up the offenses of those who had been hurt.
7. He alienated people from their authority by giving an evil report about David's leadership.
8. He offered to be the representative to make sure things were done right.
9. He would use his new position to increase his loyal following.
10. He desired acceptance and recognition as well as authority.
11. He carried out a tragic takeover of the nation with the help of those who were defiled and infected with an evil report.

"As coals are to burning coals, and wood to fire; so is a contentious man to kindle strife" (Proverbs 26:21).

Infection is responding to an evil report with human reasoning and emotion rather than with spiritual understanding and genuine love.

"A wicked doer giveth heed to false lips" (Proverbs 17:4).

- If the defilement of an evil report is not cleansed, wrong attitudes, opinions, conclusions and actions will follow— even toward very close friends: "A whisperer separateth chief friends" (Proverbs 16:28).

   A. Symptoms of Infection:
1. Believing the evil report is true
2. Forming negative opinions based on the report
3. Focusing on negative aspects of the person involved
4. Interpreting the person's words and actions as "supporting evidence"
5. Judging motives on the basis of the evil report
6. Backing away from the person in your spirit
7. Telling the evil report to others

5. **Disease**

"A wicked doer giveth heed to false lips" (Proverbs 17:4).

Disease is being mentally and emotionally controlled by the evil report and by the destructive spirit of the one who gave it to us.

"He that hateth dissembleth with his lips, and layeth up deceit within him; when he *speaketh* fair, believe him not: for there are seven abominations in his heart" (Proverbs 26:24,25).

"Thou shalt not go up and down as a *talebearer* among thy people" (Leviticus 19:16).

- A diseased Christian has grieved and quenched the Holy Spirit by taking up the offenses of others, making them his own and adding to them.

A. Symptions of disease:

1. Developing bitterness and/or rebellion, even though the person involved did not directly offend us.

2. Setting ourselves up as the judge in matters which are God's responsibility, and recruiting others to "our side."

3. Searching out evil reports and using them to give the worst possible impression: "An ungodly man diggeth up evil: and in his lips there is as a burning fire" (Proverbs 16:27).

4. Believing that such actions are actually accomplishing God's will rather than realizing that we give non-Christians occasion to blaspheme God's name because of our lack of genuine love: "I speak to your shame . . . brother goeth to law with brother, and that *before the unbelievers*. Now therefore there is utterly a fault among you . . . ye do wrong, and defraud, and that your brethren" (1 Corinthians 6:5-8).

   Often we do not act on information when we should do so because the defilement or infection hinders God's grace in us (see Hebrews 12:25).

• Attempts to restore a Christian who has been overtaken in a fault will usually fail unless the defilement of listening to evil reports is first cleansed and then replaced with the spirit of Christ's love, humility and forgiveness.

HOW TO CLEANSE OUR MINDS FROM AN EVIL REPORT

1. Ask God to cleanse your mind from the defilement of an evil report.

2. Pray for God to give you genuine love for each one involved in the evil report.

3. Cleanse your mind with appropriate Scripture:

• Have I accepted the evil report as true?

"The simple believeth every word: but the prudent man looketh well to his going" (Proverbs 14:15).

"Keep back thy servant also from presumptuous sins" (Psalm 19:13).

Presumptuousness is taking a matter for granted and assuming it to be true in the absence of proof to the contrary.

- Has the evil report affected how I feel toward the person involved?

    "A wholesome tongue is a tree of life: but perverseness therein is a breach in the spirit" (Proverbs 15:4).

    "For wherein thou judgest another, thou condemnest thyself, for thou that judgest doest the same things" (Romans 2:1).

    "Above all things have fervent love among yourselves, for love shall cover the multitude of sins" (1 Peter 4:8).

    "Love . . . thinketh no evil, rejoiceth not in iniquity" (1 Corinthians 13:5,6).

- Do I have an urge to tell someone else the evil report?

    "Let no corrupt communication proceed out of your mouth, but that which is good to the use of edifying, that it may minister grace unto the hearers" (Ephesians 4:29).

    "A talebearer revealeth secrets: but he that is of a faithful spirit concealeth the matter" (Proverbs 11:13).

    "He that covereth a transgression seeketh love; but he that repeateth a matter separateth very [close] friends" (Proverbs 17:9).

- I know my heart is clean when:

    I lose my urge to tell someone else the evil report.

    I grieve over the fact that a report was given.

    I have genuine love toward the person involved in the report.

    I am prompt to examine my own life for failures.

4. Act on what you heard:

- Is God directing you to contact the one who gave you the evil report? to ask the five questions which identify an evil report? to emphasize the importance of speaking the truth in love? (See John 17:20-26; Philippians 2:1-4.)

- Is God directing you to contact the person involved in the situation? Is God directing you to contact the person involved in the evil report in order to check out the facts and help to restore in the spirit of meekness? (See Matthew 18:15-18; Galatians 6:1.)

- Is God directing you to contact those who are spiritually responsible for the situation?

   Once they are informed, the responsibility for further action rests with them.

   Your responsibility is to continue to pray for those involved in the situation.

Animal House

The following is a list of Scriptures that provided some seed thoughts for *Kingdom Zoology*. Notice the beast-like attributes:

Philippians 3:2: Beware of *dogs*, beware of evil workers.

Matthew 7:6: Give not that which is holy unto *dogs*, neither cast ye your pearls before *swine*, lest they trample them under their feet, and turn again and rend you.

Matthew 25:33: And he [Jesus] shall set the *sheep* on his right hand, but the *goats* on the left.

Hosea 4:16: For Israel slideth back as a backsliding *heifer*.

Matthew 7:15: Beware of false prophets which come to you in *sheep's* clothing, but inwardly they are ravening *wolves*.

Matthew 10:16: Behold, I [Jesus] send you [disciples] forth as *sheep* in the midst of *wolves*: be ye therefore wise as *serpents*, and harmless as *doves*.

John 10:11-16: I [Jesus] am the good shepherd. The good shepherd giveth his life for the *sheep*. But he that is a hireling, and not the shepherd, whose own the *sheep* are not, seeth the *wolf* coming, and leaveth the *sheep*, and fleeth: and the *wolf* catcheth them, and scattereth the *sheep*. The hireling fleeth, because he is a hireling and careth not for the *sheep*. I am the good shepherd, and know my *sheep*, and am known of mine. As the Father knoweth me, even so know I the Father: and I lay down my life for the *sheep*. And other *sheep* I have, which are not of this fold: them also I must bring, and they shall hear my voice: and there shall be one fold, and one shepherd.

Acts 20:29: For I [Paul] know this, that after my departure shall grievous *wolves* enter in among you [Ephesians], not sparing the *flock*.

Matthew 3:7: But when he [Jesus] saw many of the Pharisees and Saducees come to his baptism, he said unto them, O generation of *vipers*, who hath warned you to flee from the wrath to come?

Matthew 23:33: Ye *serpents*, ye generation of *vipers*, how can ye [Pharisees] escape the damnation of hell?

Mark 14:27: And Jesus said unto them [disciples], All ye shall be offended because of me this night: for it is written, I will smite the shepherd, and the *sheep* shall be scattered.

Jeremiah 50:6: My [Jehovah] people hath been lost *sheep*: their shepherds have caused them to go astray, they have turned them away on the mountains: they have gone from mountain to hill, they have forgotten their resting places.

John 21:15: So when they had dined, Jesus saith to Simon Peter, Simon, son of Jonas, lovest thou me more than these? He saith unto him, Yea, Lord; thou knowest that I love thee. He said unto him, Feed my *lambs*.

Ezekiel 13:4: O Israel, thy prophets are like the *foxes* in the desert.

Luke 13:32: And he [Jesus] said unto them [Pharisees], Go ye and tell that *fox* [Herod], Behold, I cast out devils, and I do cures today and tomorrow, and the third day I shall be perfected.

Hebrews 13:20: Now the God of peace, that brought again from the dead our Lord Jesus, that great shepherd of the *sheep*, through the blood of the everlasting covenant.

Notes

Chapter 2

1. Donald Joy, *Bonding* (Dallas, TX: Word Publishing, 1985), pp. 5-6.

Chapter 4

1. Isaac Rehert, "Evil: Taking Possession of the Human Soul," *Baltimore Sun* (November 18, 1983), p. B4.

2. M. R. DeHaan II, *The Pharisee in Me* (Grand Rapids, MI: Radio Bible Class, 1980), p. 10.

3. A. W. Tozer, *Man: The Dwelling Place of God* (Camp Hill, PA: Christian Publications, n.d.), pp. 167-168.

4. James Strong, *Strong's Exhaustive Concordance of the Bible* (McClean, VA: MacDonald Publishing Company, n.d.), p. 1090 and p. 17.

Chapter 6

1. William Barclay, *The Letters of John and Jude* (Philadelphia, PA: The Westminster Press, 1976), p. 134.

Chapter 7

1. *Amplified Bible* (Grand Rapids, MI: Zondervan Publishing House, 1965), p. 722.

2. William Wilson, *Wilson's Old Testament Word Studies* (McLean, VA: MacDonald Publishing Company, n.d.), p. 341.

Chapter 8

1. James Strong, *Strong's Exhaustive Concordance of the Bible* (McLean, VA: MacDonald Publishing Company, n.d.), p. 929 and p. 97.

Chapter 9

1. James Strong, *Strong's Exhaustive Concordance of the Bible* (McLean, VA: MacDonald Publishing Compan;y, n.d.), p. 361 and p. 9.

2. James Dobson, *Dr. Dobson Answers Your Questions* (Wheaton, IL: Living Books, 1982), pp. 127-128.

Chapter 10

1. James Strong, *Strong's Exhaustive Concordance of the Bible* (McLean, VA: MacDonald Publishing Company, n.d.), p. 361 and p. 56.

Chapter 11

1. James Strong, *Strong's Exhaustive Concordance of the Bible* (McLean, VA: MacDonald Publishing Company, n.d.), p. 890 and p. 59.

2. Paul Van Gorder, *The Call for Church Discipline* (Grand Rapids, MI: Radio Bible Class, 1982), pp. 12-15.

3. Harold J. Brokke, *The Message of the Cross* (Minneapolis, MN: Bethany Fellowship, n.d.), p. 2.

Chapter 12

1. James Strong, *Strong's Exhaustive Concordance of the Bible* (McLean, VA: MacDonald Publishing Company, n.d.), p. 360 and p. 76.

Chapter 14

1. Charles Swindoll, *The Grace Awakening* (Dallas, TX: Word Publishing, 1990), pp. 5-6.

2. Swindoll, *The Grace Awakening,* pp. 213-214.

Chapter 15

1. W. E. Vine, *An Expository Dictionary of New Testament*

Words (Old Tappan, NJ: Fleming H. Revell Company, n.d.), p. 280.

2. W. E. Vine, *An . . . Words*, pp. 280-281 and p. 315.

3. Mark A. Pearson, *May Christians Judge?* (York, PA: Living Word Ministries, 1978), pp. 1-18.

4. "How to Guard Against the Defilement of Listening to an Evil Report" (Oak Brook, IL: Institute in Basic Life Principles, 1981), p. 4.

Chapter 16

1. Muriel James and Dorothy Jongeward, *Born to Win* (New York, NY: Signet Books, 1971), pp. 76-77.

2. James and Jongeward, *Born to Win*, p. 94.

3. Stephen B. Karpman, "Fairy Tales and Script Drama Analysis" (New York, NY: T. A. Bulletin, VII, No. 26, April 1968), pp. 39-43.

Chapter 17

1. Philip Yancey and Dr. Paul Brand, *In His Image* (Grand Rapids, MI: Zondervan Publishing House, 1984), p. 56.

2. Yancey and Brand, *In His Image*, p. 56-57.

3. "Insights From the World of 'Opportunistic' Germs on How to Protect the Body of Christ" (Oak Brook, IL: Institute in Basic Life Principles, n.d.). With permission from the Institute, I borrowed freely from this work throughout the chapter.

Chapter 18

1. Paul Zimmerman, *A Thinking Man's Guide to Pro Football* (New York, NY: Simon & Shuster, 1984), p. 12.

2. C. Truman Davis, M.D., "The Crucifixion of Jesus" (Phoenix, AZ: Arizona Medicine, March, 1965), p. 186.

3. W. E. Vine, *An Expository Dictionary of New Testament*

Words (Old Tappan, NJ: Fleming H. Revell Company, n.d.), p. 156.

4. W. E. Vine, *An . . . Words*, p. 83.

5. "Investigate Boxing?" *Parade* (October 21, 1990), p. 5.

6. W. E. Vine, *An . . . Words*, pp. 66-67.